INDIAN TRIBES OF ALBERTA

by

Hugh A. Dempsey

GLENBOW MUSEUM

1988

Glenbow Museum
130-9th Avenue SE
Calgary, Alberta, Canada, T2K 0P3

ISBN 0-919224-00-8

Contents

Introduction

No one knows when the first Indians come to Alberta, nor can the first arrivals be identified by tribe. Geologists say that Alberta once was covered by vast glaciers which made human habitation impossible. The most recent of these was the Wisconsin Glacier, which retreated about 11,000 years ago. As it melted, it left an ice-free corridor along the east slope of the Rocky Mountains through which archaeologists say small bands of natives come on their migrations from Asia. Some may have stayed in Alberta for generations while others moved south and east in search of food. The climate was similar to that of today, so hunters found plentiful numbers of buffalo and other game animals, as well as berries and roots.

Evidence regarding the life and habits of these prehistoric dwellers has been unearthed by archaeologists who have discovered campsites and hunting areas. Through scientific excavations they have determined that some sites in Alberta are at least 11,000 years old. In addition, points (or arrowheads) found on the surface or in sand blowouts are similar to those from other parts of North America also known to be that old, or older.

Prehistoric man depended upon stone, wood, bone and leather for his weapons, tools and implements. Bows and arrows or the earlier atlatls (spear throwers) were made of wood, with projectile points of chipped or flaked stone. Hammers, knives, scrapers, drills and other tools also were made of stone by these prehistoric craftsmen. Animal skins provided coverings for tepees, clothing, storage containers, and shields, while bone was used for handles, drills and personal ornaments. Wood, always a versatile product, was too fragile to survive in the sites which have been excavated, yet it is known that birchbark was used for containers and boats, lodgepole pine for tepee poles, and burls for bowls.

Other native products used by the Indians were mountain goat horns for spoons, antlers for handles, plants for food and medicine, porcupine quills for decoration, sinew for thread, and clay for pottery.

The earliest written records indicate that in the 1700s, southern Alberta was occupied by the Blackfoot, Blood, Peigan and Gros Ventre tribes, with bands of Shoshoni, Kootenay, and Crow Indians having only recently departed. The Kootenay and other transmountain tribes continued to make regular buffalo hunting expeditions into the area, while more southerly tribes came on warring raids. Along the North Saskatchewan River, the Sarcee Indians spent part of their time in the woodlands but were adapting to prairie life; north of them were their parent tribe, the Beavers, and beyond them, the Slaveys.

These Indian of Alberta felt the effects of white man's culture long before they saw their first European. When traders arrived on the shores of Hudson Bay in the late 1600s, they provided Indians with metal tools and weapons. These, in turn, were traded to inland tribes for huge profits, so that knives, kettles and other utensils gradually moved westward through intertribal trading.

Similarly, the horse had been unknown to North American Indians, the first ones arriving with the Spanish conquest of Mexico. As these animals were stolen or strayed, they were traded from tribe to tribe, reaching southern Alberta in the early 1700s.

Within a few years, the tribes close to Hudson Bay had learned to depend upon trade goods, and began to penetrate westward in search of furs to use for barter. The Crees and Assiniboines moved up the North Saskatchewan River to the mountains, driving the poorly-armed Sarcee and Blackfoot tribes south and the Beavers north to Peace River. Farther north, the Chipewyans entered the northeastern corner of Alberta, sending the defenceless Beavers back towards the mountains.

By the early 1800s, the Gros Ventres had moved out of Alberta to become a United States tribe. At about the same time, small groups of Iroquois and Ojibwa hunters were brought out from the East to work for the trading companies. Settling along the Athabasca and Peace Rivers, some intermarried with the Crees but still retained a distinctive identity. Gradually, the turmoil created by the traders' arrival settled down, and the tribes retained their existing hunting grounds until they settled on reserves near the latter part of the Nineteenth Century.

During the Nineteenth Century, the woodland tribes in particular, made major adjustments in their lives. Where previously their annual cycle had centred around animals and fish in their search for food, they now became trappers, basing their travels upon semi-annual visits to the trading posts. The prairie tribes were less influenced by the traders as trapping was not profitable on the plains. Instead, these Indians made pemmican and sold horses and buffalo robes in exchange for European products.

With the coming of the traders, life was made easier for the native hunter who could use a gun instead of a bow and arrows, while women used pots for cooking, knives for cutting meat, axes for chopping firewood, and metal-bladed scrapers for tanning.

Less welcome were the diseases from which the Indians had no immunity. Small-pox, in particular, killed thousands of people in the epidemics which swept the area. The 1837 epidemic alone wiped out two-thirds of the Blackfoot nation. Epidemics of measles and whooping cough killed many children, while insidious killers such as tuberculosis, scrofula and venereal disease carried off scores of victims. Liquor also had been unknown to the Indians of Alberta and its introduction resulted in endless misery and hardship.

Following the fur traders came the Christian missionaries, bringing a religion which they hoped would replace native beliefs and pave the way for European civilization. Tireless and dedicated men, some of them devoted their lives to mission work in Alberta. The first was Rev. Robert Rundle, a Methodist, who arrived at Fort Edmonton in 1840. He was followed a year later by Father Jean Thibault, an Oblate priest, and a few years later, Anglican missionaries reached the north. For the next half century, the mission work in Alberta was divided largely among these three faiths, some of the more notable clergymen being Father Albert Lacombe, Rev. George McDougall and his son John, Rev. Samuel Trivett, Rev. John Tims, and Bishop Emile Grouard. A particularly outstanding missionary was the Rev. Henry Bird Steinhauer, an Ojibwa Indian educated in eastern Canada, who was equally at ease speaking his native tongue or reading Greek or Latin literature.

After the western territories became part of Canada in 1870, steps were taken to negotiate treaties with the various tribes. The first such document to affect Alberta was Treaty No. Six, signed by the Crees, Assiniboines and Ojibwas at Forts Carlton and Pitt in 1876. In Alberta, it provided for the surrender of all lands in the central part of the province.

The southern limit of this treaty area was marked by a line from the Rocky Mountains along the Red Deer River to Tail Creek, then due east for 20 miles and south-east in a straight line to the mouth of the Red Deer. The northern boundary was from the source of the Red Deer River, north to Jasper House, down the Athabasca River to the town of Athabasca, due east to Lac La Biche and north-east along a line paralleling the Beaver River.

In the following year, 1877, Treaty No. Seven was signed with the Blackfoot, Blood, Peigan, Sarcee and Stoney tribes. They surrendered all lands south of Treaty Six. The northern part of Alberta was slower in being settled, with Treaty Eight not being negotiated with the Beaver, Cree, Slavey and Chipewyan Indians until 1899.

Although the terms varied in some details, most of the treaties were similar. The amount of land set aside for reserves was based upon five persons per square mile. Tools and farming implements, nets and livestock were provided. Treaty money of $5 a year was given to each Indian, with chiefs getting $25 and councillors or minor chiefs $15. Provisions also were made for health services, education and hunting rights.

By the 1880s, the buffalo were virtually exterminated and settlers began to move into Alberta. On the prairies the Indians had no recourse but to go to their reserves and to try to start a new way of life. In the north, many Indians were able to continue their old ways for two or three more decades, but finally they too had to find another way of making a living.

For the next half century, time seemed to stand still for the Indians. Children were taken away to residential schools, disease and malnutrition caused a steady decline in population, and only half-hearted efforts were made to help the Indian make the difficult transition from his old way of life.

Significant changes did not begin to occur until after World War Two. Then, with the improvement of health services, better education and, most importantly, the involvement of Indians in political activism, their situation gradually improved. During the 1950s and 1960s, the Indians received the right to vote, liquor privileges, integrated education, and economic development programs. In the 1970s and 1980s, there was a rapid trend towards Indians assuming responsibility for self-government, and fighting a long bitter battle for a place in the Canadian Constitution. Self-government has also created problems, with some reserves experiencing serious financial crises because of their inexperience in handling their own tribal funds. However, leaders point out that the government never before permitted the Indians to have responsibilities, so it is necessary for them to learn by their own mistakes. This appears to be happening, as tribal deficits have caused layoffs, cutbacks, and the voting out of the offending councillors at subsequent elections — just as any concerned voters would do. In spite of administrative changes, the primary occupations of Indians have continued to be farming, ranching, fishing, trapping, and logging.

These years marked a period of cultural awareness, as pow-wows, cultural centres, museums, Indian studies programs at universities, and Indian-directed media all worked towards the preservation of native language and traditions. This came at a time of a rapidly expanding population (the largest birth rate of any racial group in Canada), serious social problems, and a major movement of Indians from reserves to the cities.

The transition has not been easy, nor is it over. It had been filled with bitterness, confusion and heartache. For some, the battle has been won, but for many others, difficult years lie ahead as Indians find their place in Canadian society.

BLACKFOOT NATION

Over the years, the name "Blackfoot" has become associated with the famous tribes of North America. Together with the Sioux, Iroquois, Apache and Comanche, they have gained the reputation of being a great warlike nation that for a time successfully coped with the invasion of the white man. As early as 1841, Sir George Simpson spoke of the Blackfoot as a "very interesting people who have excited more curiosity than any other of the native tribes of North America."

The Blackfoot nation consists primarily of three tribes, the Bloods, Blackfoot and Peigans, all of whom speak the same language, and are of Algonkian linguistic stock. Allied to them are the Sarcee Indians, who speak a different tongue, and the Gros Ventres who, until 1861, also were part of the confederacy. However, in that year a dispute over stolen horses turned them into bitter enemies.

The Blackfoot, in their own language, refer to themselves as *Soyi-tapi,* or Prairie People. An older term *Nitsi-tapi,* or Real People, was once a name for themselves but is now used to describe any Indian person, regardless of tribe.

There are a number of myths told about the origin of the Blackfoot nation. One of the most common states that the group was being harrassed by enemies on all sides, so they decided to split into three camps to guard their frontiers. One group went to the north to guard against the Crees, another to the southwest to fight the mountain tribes, and the third to the southeast to guard against the Crows, Assiniboines and Sioux. Some time later, a man from the northern tribe went to visit the other two and on the way he passed an area that had been ravaged by a prairie fire. When he arrived at the southeast camp, he asked for the chief, and everyone he spoke to claimed he was the chief. As a result, the man called them the tribe of Many Chiefs *(Akainai),* which became the basis for the word Kainai, the native term for the Bloods.

In turn, the people noticed the traveller's blackened moccasins and called his tribe the Blackfoot, *(Sik-sikah').*

When the man went to the third camp, he found that the women had become lazy and were not tanning their hides properly. As a result, some of the men wore robes which had dried bits of meat and hair still attached. The visitor thus called the tribe Scabby Hides *(Apikuni),* this word later being corrupted into the name Peigan.

According to early explorers, the Blackfoot came to the plains from the woodland regions of central Saskatchewan, although when they were met by the first white man, they retained no features of a woodland culture. By this time they were plains Indians who followed the buffalo and lived by the hunt. In fact, if there was a woodland origin, it was completely forgotten by the tribe, for even Crowfoot, the great chief, knew nothing about it. In speaking to a visitor he was "very positive in asserting that his people for generations past has always lived in the same part of the country that they now inhabit. He entirely scorned the idea that they had come from the east."

The Blackfoot did not see a white man until the mid-1700s, but by then they already knew about him and his inventions. When the first traders arrived on the shores of Hudson Bay in the 1600s, they bartered metal objects, beads and other items to the local Indians. These passed from tribe to tribe until they reached the plains. Such utensils as

Artist Karl Bodmer sketched this Blackfoot Indian on horseback in 1833. At that time, the Blackfoot controlled a vast territory from the North Saskatchewan to the Missouri River.

knives, axes and pots were bought by the Blackfoot from other Indians by paying huge prices for them. One Blackfoot also described to explorer David Thompson when they used the first guns against the unsuspecting Shoshonis.

> The War Chief was close to us, anxious to see the effect of our guns. The lines were too far asunder for us to make a sure shot, and we requested him to close the line to about sixty yards, which was gradually done, and lying flat on the ground behind the shields, we watched our opportunity when they drew their bows to shoot at us, their bodies were then exposed and each of us, as opportunity offered, fired with deadly aim, and either killed, or severely wounded, every one we aimed at.

It was during this period, probably between 1700 and 1725, that the Blackfoot also obtained their first horses. These were descendents of those brought by the Spaniards when they had invaded Mexico. Over the years, animals had been acquired by the southern tribes and were passed northward. David Thompson's story teller related how "our enemies the Snake Indians and their allies had Misstutin (Big Dogs, that is Horses) on which they rode, swift as the Deer, on which they dashed at the Peeagans, and with their stone Pukamoggan (clubs) knocked them on the head."

By the time Anthony Henday first met the Blackfoot tribes in 1754, they already were skilled horsemen and were adequately supplies with guns, kettles and knives. As a result, Henday could not persuade them to travel many miles through enemy territory to visit the trading posts on Hudson Bay. By the late 1700s, however, the companies were moving inland and trading directly with the plains tribes. The Blackfoot were not trappers so their main trade with the white people consisted of dried meat, buffalo robes and horses.

9

Two leading chiefs of the Blackfoot nation, Bull Back Fat (left) and Bear Chief (centre) were sketched in 1833 with a Kootenay Indian, Homach-ksachkum, who had come across the mountains to trade.

Because of the lack of fur in Blackfoot hunting grounds, the early traders had no reason to build forts there. Instead, such posts as Fort George, Edmonton House and Rocky Mountain House were constructed along the Saskatchewan River where they could serve the plains tribes but not actually be among them. In this way, the daily lives of the plains Indians were not directly affected like those in the north who were encouraged to become trappers and hunters for the trading companies.

As a result, the Blackfoot were able to develop a complex society based upon the buffalo for food and the horse for mobility. Before the availability of European objects, the Blackfoot had travelled in small bands, using dogs to haul their travois. But with the introduction of the horse, they found it easier to pursue the buffalo and to carry on their skirmishes with enemy tribes. The availability of food during this period gave them more time to devote to religious societies, decorative arts and warfare. It also enabled them to gather into larger bands which gave the whole nation a strong sense of unity.

At this time, the Blackfoot had three main methods of hunting buffalo. The most ancient method was the use of the *piskun* or buffalo jump. This was usually a steep cliff where the buffalo were driven over and those not killed by the fall were shot in the corrals built at the bottom. Another method was the surround, where hunters crept close to a small herd and picked off the best animals one by one as the others milled around. The third, and most exciting method, was the chase, where men on their best running horses pursued a stampeding herd and shot the animals at close range.

To the Blackfoot, the buffalo was the staff of life. The meat provided food; the skin was used for clothing and tepee covers; the bones were used for handles, needles, and other utensils; the horns were made into spoons, the rawhide was made into bags; and even the tail was used as a fly whisk or for sprinkling water on hot stones in the sweat bath. It is not surprising, therefore, that the Blackfoot considered the buffalo to be a holy animal, a gift to them from the Sun. As a result, many of their religious ceremonies paid special tribute to the buffalo, and whenever an albino buffalo was killed, its hide was left as an offering to the Sun. When the vast herds were slaughtered by hide hunters in 1880-81, many older men believed the animals had been driven into a hole in the ground by the Sun, who was angry at the way they were being destroyed.

Soon after the Blackfoot received guns and horses, they began a valiant struggle to retain their hunting grounds. From the north and east, the better armed Crees and Assiniboines were constantly moving in on their territory, while to the west, the Kootenays and other mountain tribes made regular expeditions onto the plains in search of buffalo. This meant that the Blackfoot tribes were constantly on the alert ready to protect their lands.

At the time of the arrival of the earliest British traders, the Blackfoot confederacy controlled a vast area bounded on the west by the Rocky Mountains, on the north by the North Saskatchewan River, on the south by the Missouri River, and on the east by the present Alberta-Saskatchewan boundary. Within that area, a fur trader in 1815 said that the Peigans controlled all the hunting grounds within a hundred miles of the mountains; the Bloods were between the Red Deer and Bow Rivers; the Blackfoot were north of them; the Sarcees between Red Deer and Battle River east to Beaverhills Lake; and the Gros Ventres were south of the Bloods and east of the Peigans.

Within a few years, however, all tribes had moved farther south under the pressure of Cree and Assiniboine raids. By the middle of the century, the Peigans had broadened their area in Montana but had retreated south of the Bow River; the Bloods were down to the Lethbridge-Sweetgrass Hills area; the Blackfoot centred upon Blackfoot Crossing and Red Deer River; the Gros Ventres were in the Cypress Hills area and southward, while the Sarcees were along the Red Deer River.

However, the tribes did not entirely abandon the northern area, for as late as 1841, Sir George Simpson indicated that

Blackfoot horses and travois were sketched near Fort Macleod in the 1870s by Mounted Policeman R. B. Nevitt.

the Saskatchewan River was the dividing line between the Blackfoot and Cree between Fort Pitt and Edmonton.

Although the southern part of their hunting grounds extended into the present United States, the Blackfoot did not welcome the Americans. This attitude developed because the first Americans in the Lewis and Clark expedition killed a Peigan Indian in 1806. The situation was further aggravated by the different fur gathering methods used by the Americans and British. In the north, British traders established forts and encouraged the Indians to bring in their furs and robes to barter. In the south, American mountain men and trappers caught their own furs and avoided any dealings with the Indians. To the Blackfoot, these men were stealing from them, and were treated as enemies.

This situation existed until 1831, when the American Fur Company made peace with the Blackfoot tribes and built Fort Piegan on the upper waters of the Missouri. From that time on, the Blackfoot developed into keen traders who pitted American against British in order to get the best prices for their robes and furs.

The population of the Blackfoot tribes varied over the years, being affected by tragic epidemics of smallpox and other diseases. In the table below are figures given by Alexander Henry in 1809. Fort Edmonton traders in 1823, George Catlin in 1832, Sir George Simpson in 1841, James Doty in 1854, and U.S. General Alfred Sully in 1870. All were listed by lodges, but a fairly accurate population can be determined by estimating eight persons per tepee. Particularly noticeable is the drastic decline in population after the smallpox epidemic of 1837.

The first major change in Blackfoot relations with the whites occurred in 1855 when a treaty was signed with the American government. At this time the United States was considering building a railroad across the West and wanted to obtain clear title to Indian lands. In the treaty, the tribes surrendered the major part of Montana in exchange for an exclusive hunting grounds, annuity payments and other benefits. Signing this treaty were 14 Peigans, eight Bloods, and four Blackfoot. Although the leading Peigan chiefs were there, many of the Bloods and Blackfoot did not attend as they lived almost exclusively in the British part of their hunting grounds and had no interest in an American treaty.

Within a few years after this event, white people began trickling into Montana. First there were a few free traders and missionaries, then the discovery of gold along the mountains brought a flood of gold seekers, merchants and ranchers.

The influx resulted in a number of clashes between Indian and white man, reaching such proportions by 1866 that

BLACKFOOT POPULATION

	Blackfoot	Blood	Peigan	Estimated Population
1809 -----	200 tents	100 tents	350 tents	5,200
1823 -----	500 tents	300 tents	550 tents	10,800
1832 -----	450 tents	450 tents	750 tents	13,200
1841 -----	300 tents	250 tents	350 tents	7,200
1854 -----	290 tents	270 tents	290 tents	6,800
1870 -----	226 tents	212 tents	330 tents	6,144

Many tragedies occurred after Americans built Fort Whoop-Up in southern Alberta in 1869. With whiskey as its main stock in trade, it caused untold misery and destruction during its five years of operation.

Montanans were referring to the troubles as a "Blackfoot war." The events over the next few years finally culminated with an attack by the U.S. cavalry, under the direction of Major Eugene Baker, upon a peaceful camp of Peigans. The soldiers were looking for Mountain Chief's camp, where they expected to find a number of men wanted for murder, but by mistake they attacked the camp of Heavy Runner, killing 173 men, women and children. This event, which occurred in January 1870, became known as the Baker massacre.

This incident drove many of the Indians to the Canadian side of the border, for they feared the Americans intended to wipe out the entire nation. But even there, they were not free of the evils of the frontier. In 1869, free traders discovered they could sell whiskey in southern Alberta and Saskatchewan without fear of being arrested by Canadian or U.S. authorities.

During the first winter of 1869-70, a fort was built near the present city of Lethbridge, and was so successful that within a short time others dotted the region. Such places as Fort Whoop-Up, Standoff, Slideout, Spitzee, Elbow River, Lafayette French's and Farwell's Post sold whiskey and other goods.

The demoralization of the tribes was rapid. In one winter, 70 Bloods were killed in drunken quarrels at just one of the posts. Father Scollen, an Oblate priest, described the situation. "The fiery water flowed as freely," he said, "as the streams running from the Rocky Mountains, and hundreds of the poor Indians fell victims to the white man's craving for money, some poisoned, some frozen to death whilst in a state of intoxication, and many shot down by American bullets."

Within a short time, the Blackfoot tribes were impoverished and demoralized. However, assistance finally came

13

from the Canadian government in 1874 when the newly-formed North-West Mounted Police came west and stamped out the illegal traffic. Within a short time the Blackfoot began to rebuild their shattered lives, replenish their horse herds, and regain their status as lords of the plains.

But just as peace with American authorities had resulted in an influx of settlers, so did Canadians begin moving into Blackfoot hunting grounds. First, tiny villages arose beside the forts built by the Mounted Police, then a number of small ranches and farms were established nearby. The Blackfoot, alarmed by this action, petitioned the government in 1876 and a year later the Blackfoot Treaty was made.

In this agreement the Blackfoot surrendered all of southern Alberta to the Canadian government in exchange for reserves based upon five people per square mile. It also gave them annuity payments, and other benefits.

By this time, the Blackfoot nation was effectively split in two. The South Peigans, living almost entirely in the United States, looked upon their large reservation on Birch and Two Medicine Creeks as their home, while the North Peigans, Blackfoot and Bloods lived on the Canadian side. At the time of treaty they did not give much thought to reserves, but by the time the buffalo had been destroyed in 1880, the Blackfoot had decided to settle at Blackfoot Crossing, 100 km (60 miles) east of Calgary; the Bloods between the St. Mary and Belly Rivers, south of Fort Macleod; and the North Peigans on the Oldman River, 25 km (15 miles) west of Fort Macleod.

From that time on, each tribe developed according to its own situation. In some cases this depended upon the fertility of the soil, while in others it was affected by the capabilities of its leaders, the calibre of Indian Department employees, and relationships with surrounding farmers and ranchers. The histories of the Blackfoot, Blood and Peigan after 1880, then, are different from the common heritage and history they shared during the nomadic period. Following chapters will deal with each tribe separately after they settled on their reserves.

The Blackfoot were famous as warriors and horsemen. Notice that one of the horses is wearing a face shield.

BLACKFOOT TRIBE

Throughout history the Blackfoot has been one of the most famous and respected tribes in Canada. Being the northernmost of the three tribes that made up the Blackfoot nation, they were the first ones to meet the fur traders, and, as a result, the entire Blackfoot nation was named after them. After they settled on their reserve, the Canadian Pacific Railway passed nearby, so that the name of the tribe became well known to Canadian travellers.

However, it was probably their great leader, Crowfoot, who brought much of the fame to his tribe. A respected diplomat and orator, his actions in turning down an invitation to join Sitting Bull against the Americans in 1876, his dominant role in the Blackfoot Treaty of 1877, and his decision not to take part in the Riel Rebellion of 1885, made him and his tribe famous throughout the world.

When the Blackfoot joined with the Bloods, Peigans, Sarcees and Stoneys to sign a treaty with the Canadian government in 1877, the Indians still were in control of southern Alberta. The buffalo were plentiful and the Blackfoot had their independence and freedom.

Some of the chiefs were opposed to making a treaty, for there was a feeling that any agreements with the white man would end in disaster. They pointed out how their neighbours in Montana had made a treaty in 1855, but it had been broken again and again by the Americans. In addition, they said that whenever a treaty was made, enemy Indians and white men flooded into the surrounding lands.

However, largely due to the feeling of trust established with the North-West Mounted Police, the tribes decided to sign. Crowfoot made it clear why they were taking this move. "If the Police had not come to the country," he said, "where would we all be now? Bad men and whiskey were killing us so fast that very few, indeed, of us would have been left today.

The Police have protected us as the feathers of the bird protect it from the frosts of winter."

The three head chiefs who signed the treaty for the Blackfoot were Crowfoot, Old Sun, and Old Sun's younger brother, Heavy Shield. Signing as minor chiefs were Eagle Rib, Low Horn, Bear Shield, Bull Elk, Big Plume, Calf Robe, Running Rabbit, White Eagle, Weasel Calf, Rabbit Carrier, Eagle and Eagle White Calf. A few days later, Three Bulls, Crowfoot's foster brother, signed an adhesion to the treaty. When the agreement was made, a total of 1,515 Blackfoot received annuity payments, although a number of families were away hunting. In 1878, 1,946 Blackfoot were paid and in 1879 there were 2,249.

The chiefs decided to take a reserve on the Bow River, centred at Blackfoot Crossing, south of the present village of Cluny. Originally they were to share a common reserve with the Bloods and Sarcees, but the two other tribes later decided to move farther away.

The first survey of the reserve took place in 1878, and again in 1883, at which time 470 square miles of land were set aside for the tribe. Particular emphasis was placed on reserving coal deposits which had been found near Blackfoot Crossing, for the government saw these as future source of income for the tribe.

But the sole interest of the Blackfoot was in buffalo hunting. This great shaggy beast had been the source of life for the tribe for countless generations, and at the time the treaty was signed, the government had predicted the buffalo would last for at least another ten years. However, just as some of the chiefs had predicted, bad luck came to the tribe after the treaty. Within a few months, three of the nation's leading chiefs had died. According to Father Scollen, these deaths "alarmed them considerably, and was looked upon as a very bad omen for the future."

Then, during the winter of 1877-78, prairie fires raced across the Blackfoot hunting grounds, driving the buffalo far to the south and east. By the following summer, some of the people were beginning to starve, and everyone could see that the buffalo had almost all been destroyed. At last, in a futile effort to hold onto their freedom, the Blackfoot followed the last buffalo herds into Montana and remained there from the fall of 1879 until the spring of 1881. When they returned to Canada, the last buffalo had been killed, and the Blackfoot were starving and confused. Some people blamed the treaty for wiping out the buffalo; others said that the Sun spirit had opened a hole in the ground and driven the buffalo into it because he was angry at the Indians for letting the white people come in.

With the buffalo gone, the Blackfoot's old way of life was destroyed. There was no alternative for them but to go to their newly-surveyed reserve and to accept the rations of beef and flour given out by the government.

The next years which followed were frustrating and disillusioning. Small log houses replaced tepees and the chiefs were encouraged to start a new life as farmers and gardeners. There was no particular enthusiasm for this strange kind of work, but gradually the gardens of potatoes, turnips and grain increased along the bottoms of the Bow River valley. In 1882, Old Sun was encouraged to move upstream to a new campsite, where a ration

house was built for his band. Over the years, his area was known as North Camp, while that near Blackfoot Crossing was called South Camp.

In the following year, 1883, the main line of the Canadian Pacific Railway passed along the northern boundary of the reserve, and stations were built at Cluny and Gleichen. Although the Blackfoot had been told the railway would be of great help to them in bringing food to their reserve, it was also a source of concern. Trains belched clouds of sparks from their pot-bellied smokestacks, setting fire to thousands of acres of the prairie grass. In addition, Indian horses wandered onto the right-of-way, and were killed by passing trains.

In spite of these problems, the Blackfoot tried to adjust to their new life. Although drought or early frosts often hit their tiny gardens, small crops of potatoes, and other vegetables were harvested. In 1884, for example, the Blackfoot Reserve had 235 acres under cultivation and the Indians produced 5,856 bushels of potatoes, 2,590 of turnips, 240 of onions, 97 of carrots, and 89 of peas. Although they planted 66 acres of wheat and 27 acres of oats, no figures were given on the harvest, although the Indian Agent reported that "wheat was the only article really good on this reserve."

As soon as the vegetables and grain had been harvested, the Blackfoot rations of beef and flour were cut in half.

During the Riel Rebellion of 1885, great fear was expressed that the Blackfoot would join in the battle. Even the famous missionary, Father Lacombe, was worried and commented: "From the beginning of the war, one who knows the Indian character could very easily perceive they were not pleased when told of the victories of the whites; on the contrary they were sorry and disappointed. Crowfoot received into his camp and fed for months many Cree families, and was very

Crowfoot, great chief of the Blackfoot, was surrounded by his thriving family in this 1884 photograph. Within six years, however, almost all of them had died from tuberculosis and other diseases.

much displeased when we tried to send away the Crees."

However, Crowfoot decided not to join the insurgents, for in the previous year he had visited the city of Winnipeg, and realized how many soldiers could be raised against them. To avoid certain defeat of his people, he decided to remain at peace.

The supression of the Riel Rebellion destroyed any hope that Indians might have held about independence. In the years that followed, they settled down to the routine of farming and gardening. By 1889, steps had been taken to open the first coal mine, and in 1895 a few cattle were exchanged for Indian cayuses to begin a ranching industry.

The death of Crowfoot in 1890, ended the great era of Blackfoot glory. Although he was followed by such men as Three Bulls, Running Rabbit, Yellow Horse and Duck Chief, none of them gained the international reputation of their first leader. Instead, the Indian

Agent was the dominant figure on the reserve and remained in this role until the 1960s.

By 1900, the main sources of income for the Blackfoot were farming, gardening, ranching, haying and coal mining. By this time a number of individually-operated mine shafts had been opened, and coal was being sold to nearby villagers and farmers.

In the meantime, the Anglicans and Roman Catholics opened missions on the reserve in 1883, the former going to North Camp and the latter to South Camp. Both denominations opened small day schools during the 1880s, and by 1889 the Anglicans had a girls' home in operation. Major residential schools had been added by the turn of the century while older students were sent away to industrial schools at Dunbow and Calgary.

A major change in the life of the Blackfoot occurred in 1910, when they were encouraged to sell part of their reserve.

With the destruction of the buffalo herds, the Blackfoot became dependent upon rations for survival. This sketch was made in their ration house in the 1880s.

The first sales consisted of lands for putting an irrigation canal through the reserve and later in 1910 for a railway line to Carseland. By this time hundreds of settlers were pouring into the west, the best lands were taken up by the homesteaders, and people began looking at the vast acres of unused lands on various reserves. Because the Indian population had been decreasing through disease and poor health conditions, many believed the Indians should sell their excess land to settlers.

The Blackfoot agreed to give up almost half of their reserve lying south of the river, and in 1912, 60,771 acres were auctioned for $941,872. Another sale was held in 1918, when 55,327 acres brought in $1,276,190. Other small parcels also were sold during this period.

The immediate result of these sales was to make the Blackfoot the wealthiest tribe in Canada and to give them a prosperity unknown to other reserves. New frame houses complete with stables and outbuildings were constructed throughout the reserve. These were fitted with stoves, tables, chairs, beds and bedding, and wells were dug nearby. In addition, roads were graded, steam engines and farming equipment purchased, and granaries built. Part of the funds were also used to build a hospital, to hire farm instructors, to provide weekly rations for the entire tribe, to provide assistance loans to farmers, and to provide an annual cash annuity.

With assistance being given to agriculture, this enterprise expanded greatly over the years, and a number of Blackfoot became successful farmers and ranchers. By 1939, there were 11,705 acres under cultivation while 114 Indian ranchers owned about 3,000 head of cattle. In addition, large areas were leased and at least 5,000 acres were brought under irrigation.

Other Indians continued to earn money through haying, coal mining, working for the band and for nearby ranchers. Of these pursuits, mining proved to be the most rewarding, particularly after the reorganization of production methods in

1931. Modern equipment enabled production to reach about 10,000 tons a year and provided a seasonal income for some 50 families. However, after World War Two, the availability of natural gas and competition from other areas gradually narrowed the markets, until the Blackfoot mines were finally closed.

World War Two also changed the entire Blackfoot economy. Although income from leases had enabled the tribe to maintain band funds of over $3 million, the rapid increase in the coast of living after the war quickly ate up the huge fund. In addition, improvements in health service doubled the population of the tribe between 1939 and the late 1950s. This placed a heavy drain on band funds to meet the elaborate welfare program which the tribe had established.

Step by step, the Blackfoot retrenched. Their hospital was turned over to the government in 1950, food and money payments were eliminated, and by 1958 the head chief announced they were broke and "the Blackfoot has either got to get up out of his chair or go to sleep altogether."

The result was a gradual change from tribally-funded programs to practises similar to those used on other reserves. Many individuals found farming to be too expensive and leased their lands to outsiders. The tribe also tried a number of economic development programs, some successful, some not. These included a beef cooperative, potato-growing industry, furniture plant, boat manufacturing firm, and a summer resort facility. In addition, ways of strip mining and developing their vast coal resources have been explored.

In recent years, a junior college and trade school have been established, a cultural centre developed, and a townsite laid out. The tribal council has assumed much of the responsibility for administration of the reserve and has its own native staff of office workers, counsellors, work crews, educators, and social workers. Like other reserves, the population is expanding rapidly, from 800 in 1939 to 3,560 by 1986. As a result, overcrowding has been added to the list of problems confronting the Blackfoot people.

The Anglican and Roman Catholic missionaries opened schools on the Blackfoot Reserves in the 1880s. This is an Anglican classroom about 1900.

A group of Blackfoot prepares for the first Calgary Stampede parade in 1912. At right is their head chief, Duck Chief.

In 1886, leading chiefs of the Blackfoot nation were taken on a tour of eastern Canada. Here, left to right, are One Spot and Red Crow, of the Blood tribe, and North Axe, of the North Peigans. They are accompanied by their interpreter, Jean L'Heureux.

20

BLOOD TRIBE

When the Blood Indians were invited to negotiate a treaty with the Canadian government in 1877, they were the largest tribe in what is now southern Alberta. As part of the Blackfoot nation, they had a population of about 2,200 people, including some 550 warriors.

But they almost didn't come.

The Bloods, like other members of the nation, were worried about the influx of settlers, traders and Metis into their hunting grounds. They wanted an agreement and were anxious to discuss the subject with representatives of Queen Victoria. Accordingly, the government agreed to have a treaty session at Fort Macleod, as it was easily accessible to all tribes. However, Crowfoot did not want to meet in a white man's fort and demanded that the site be moved to Blackfoot Crossing, on the Bow River. When the government approved, the Bloods became angry, claiming that Blackfoot Crossing was solely within Blackfoot territory and would be a great inconvenience to the Bloods, Peigans and Sarcees. However, the government had made up its mind and would not budge.

On October 17th, 1877, the negotiations were ready to begin. The Stoneys, enemies of the Blackfoot, were camped across the river, and the Blackfoot and Sarcees were present in force. But just a few Peigans were in attendance and the only Blood chief present was Medicine Calf, a warrior who was noted for his distrust of the white man. The commissioners and Crowfoot were concerned that the Bloods would boycott the treaty but at last, after two days of waiting, the tribe finally arrived. Their great chief Red Crow immediately went into conference with Crowfoot and decided that because the Blackfoot chief had been there since the beginning, he would be the spokesman for them all.

On Sept. 22nd, Crowfoot accepted the terms of the treaty. Red Crow also arose and spoke to the assembly, saying "Three years ago, when the Police first came to the country, I met and shook hands with *Stamixotokon* (Col. Macleod) at Belly River. Since that time he made me many promises. He kept them all — not one of them was ever broken. Everything that the police have done has been good. I entirely trust *Stamixotokon,* and will leave everything to him. I will sign with Crowfoot."

Those who signed for the Blood tribe were head chiefs Red Crow and Rainy Chief, and minor chiefs Medicine Calf, (also called Button Chief), Bad Head (also called Father of Many Children), Hind Bull, Many Spotted Horses, Eagle Rib, Bull Backfat, White Striped Dog, Stolen Person, White Antelope, Wolf Collar, Heavily Whipped, Moon, Eagle Head, Weasel Bull, White Calf, One Spot, Eagle Shoe, Bull Turn Round and Going to the Bear. At the actual treaty payments, 2,058 persons were entered on the books, although a number of bands were missing. In 1878 there were 2,488 at the treaty payments and 3,071 in 1879.

At the treaty, the Bloods and others gave up their rights to their hunting grounds in exchange for a reserve based on five persons per square mile, as well as other benefits. Among these were the "right to pursue their vocations of hunting throughout the tract surrendered . . . subject to such regulations as may . . . be made by the Government"; to pay annual treaty of $5 to each person, $15 to minor

This was the first mission house built on the Blood Reserve. Photographed about 1885, it shows three Anglican missionaries, left to right, Samuel Trivett, John W. Tims, and George McKay, with a group of Bloods.

chiefs, and $25 to head chiefs; to receive a bonus of $12 at the original treaty; to have their share of $2,000 a year for ammunition; a uniform every three years for chiefs; a Winchester rifle, flag and medal for chiefs at the treaty signing; to send teachers among them; and to provide certain farming tools and cattle.

The government had expected that the Indians could live off the buffalo for another ten years, but events moved too quickly. In 1878 a devastating prairie fire swept across the territory, driving the buffalo herds into Montana. By the following spring the entire Blood tribe had crossed the line and was engaged in the last great buffalo hunt. Then it was all over. Starving and bewildered, the Bloods began drifting back to Canada early in 1880 and camped near Fort Macleod.

In their 1877 treaty, they had agreed to take a reserve on a miserable piece of land, four miles wide, that extended downstream from Blackfoot Crossing to the Medicine Hat area, passing through one of the driest regions of Alberta. Now that the reality of settling on a reserve faced them, they decided that they wanted to live in their usual winter camping area along the Belly River. Accordingly, officials approved the move and in 1883, a new treaty was made in which the Bloods took a reserve between the Belly and St. Mary rivers. This is the reserve the Bloods have today, approximately 352,600 acres, making it the largest reserve in Canada.

As in their nomadic life, the Bloods settled in bands along the Belly River, strung out all the way from the old whiskey fort of Slideout upstream to Big Bend. Cottonwood log houses were built to replace the worn tepees and efforts were made to break the land. By 1882, about 250 acres were broken and a few of the interested chiefs had encouraged their people to plant turnips and potatoes to supplement their meagre rations. In the fall, some 70,000 pounds of potatoes were turned over to the government root houses with much more being kept for food. The turnips were also successful.

The government was frankly surprised at the willingness of the warlike Bloods to take up farming. Former warriors seemed anxious to provide for their families and not to rely on government handouts. Such leaders as Ermine Horses, Bull Back Fat, Medicine Calf and Red Crow gave their support to the program and soon wheat, oats, barley and vegetables were added to the list of crops in the tiny gardens.

Generally speaking, the Bloods made good progress during the 1880s, considering the tremendous change which occurred in their daily lives. Rev. Samual Trivett, Anglican missionary, arrived in 1880 and opened day schools in several camps. He was followed by Methodist John Maclean, who finally turned his mission over to the Anglicans, and by Father Emile Legal, a Roman Catholic missionary, who arrived in 1887.

But all the Bloods had not simply been transformed into peaceful farmers. There was still a fierce pride and independence among them. For example, in 1882, a war party of Crees from the Cypress Hills came to the reserve and stole 45 horses. In retaliation, White Calf gathered more than 200 warriors and crossed a hundred miles of barren land to the Mounted Police post at Fort Walsh. With the help of the police, most of the horses were recovered but before the Bloods left the hills they raided a Cree camp and killed at least one of the enemy.

There were many other incidents, particularly when young warriors knew they could go on horse raiding expeditions into Montana and not be punished if they could get back to Canada. These activities gave the Bloods an air of freedom and arrogance which was lacking in some of the neighbouring tribes. It was so noticeable that one Mounted Policeman commented irritably that "the Bloods think that they are the cream of creation, and it is time for them to begin to imbibe some modification of the idea."

This pride also had its advantages, for when the Riel rebellion erupted in 1885, the Bloods gave no thought to joining.

The centre of government authority over the Blood Indians for many years was the Indian Agency, seen here about 1890.

After the Bloods settled on their reserve, they continued to live in tepees during the summer months. These traditional dwellings were much healthier than their tiny cabins.

Because of their pride, they did not consider themselves inferior to the white man and did not harbour the hatred prevalent among tribes which had suffered under the callous yoke of government administration. To the Bloods, the Crees were still their traditional enemies. In fact, a chief named Bull Shield went to the Indian Agent when he learned about the rebellion and said, "Give us ammunition and grub and we'll how you how soon we can set the Crees afoot and lick them!"

But the 1880s also were difficult for the Bloods. The death rate was extremely high and such diseases as scrofula, eresipelas, and tuberculosis were rampant. The dank, smoky cabins and meagre rations reduced the strength of the people so that every epidemic of influenza, measles, or whooping cough resulted in dozens of deaths. The year 1884, with 126 deaths and eight births, is typical of that decade. From a population of 2,488 in 1878, the tribe was reduced to 1,776 by 1885, and 1,111 by 1920. From this low point it began a steady increase as medical and economic conditions improved. By 1985 the tribe had a population of 6,342.

By the 1890s, the Bloods had become accustomed to their sedentary life. Intertribal horse raiding had almost disappeared, but they still carried on many features of their religion, including the Sun Dance, medicine pipe dances, secret societies, and a belief in the power of the Sun Spirit.

The big change in their economic routine occurred in 1894 when the first Indian-owned cattle were introduced. Horses were symbols of wealth, so there was some surprise when four of the leaders agreed to exchange some of their cayuses for "worthless" cattle. Red Crow and Crop Eared Wolf each took fifteen head and Blackfoot Old Woman and Sleeps on Top took ten head each, to form the nucleus of the Blood cattle industry. Looking after cattle was in some ways similar to their old life. A man felt at home in the saddle riding after four-legged creatures, and so the enterprise prospered. Others followed the lead of the four beginners and by 1900 the Bloods owned almost 1,500 head of cattle.

Individual initiative also became evident during this period. In 1891, a Blood named Chief Moon took a contract to provide forty tons of hay to the Mounted Police. He borrowed some equipment and with his profits soon purchased a mower of his own. During the next few years he became a regular hay contractor, competing with white men to supply the police and local ranchers.

In 1892, Heavy Gun obtained permission to open a coal mine in St. Mary River. He took a contract to supply the Indian Agency with 100 tons and proceeded to hire Indian teamsters and workers. Under the most primitive pick-and-shovel conditions they mined 14 tons a week and hauled it to the Agency. Heavy Gun later took contracts to supply the local mission and others. Two years later he sold out to Black Horse, who, together with his son Chief Mountain, continued to operate the mine for more than 30 years. During this time they supplied coal to the Indian Agency, missions, local ranchers and to householders in nearby towns.

Other Indians began cutting logs and freighting, working for local ranchers and hunting, while still others were hired by the Agency as mail carriers, scouts and interpreters.

While the land had been broken for gardens as early as 1881, these were only small plots along the river bottoms. It was not until 1907 that the first major attempt was made to bring the Bloods onto the broad prairie lands. In that year the Bloods bought a large steam ploughing outfit and families were urged to go into farming in a big way. Farming instructors were hired and by 1916 the Bloods were producing 65,000 bushels of wheat, 27,000 bushels of barley and 7,600 tons of hay without outside help.

The introduction of farming was just in time, for pressures were strong for the Bloods to surrender parts of their reserve to land-hungry farmers. This came at the height of immigration from Europe, and promoters in Cardston, Fort Macleod and Lethbridge could visualize hundreds

After the turn of the century, the Bloods began farming on the open prairies. Above is a steam tractor used for breaking land and other farming activities on the reserve.

Blood students march from dormitory to classroom at the Anglican mission school about 1916.

of settlers being placed on the reserve if it was thrown open for settlement.

The Bloods showed no interest, however. When white men came to him about giving up the land, Crop Eared Wolf, the head chief, reached down and took a bunch of grass in one hand and some soil in the other. "This you can buy from us," he said, holding up the grass and then pressing the other hand to his heart, he said, "but this soil is for me and my people forever."

Not satisfied, the government in 1907 forced the Bloods to vote on the surrender of 2,400 acres of land on the southern limit of the reserve. The result was more than three to one against the surrender, and an angry newspaper in Macleod blamed the head chief. It said the proceedings "were opposed tooth and nail by Crop Eared Wolf, the head chief. He personally canvassed every vote on the reserve. Some he scared, others he coaxed, and others he induced to stay away."

The government tried again in 1917 when it wanted Indian lands for soldier resettlement. Again the Bloods voted against the move. Then a third vote was forced upon them in 1918 and was passed by a small margin. However, the head chief charged the government with "fraud, bribery and intimidation" and the surrender was never ratified.

Once farming and ranching were well established, the Bloods began a steady development, hampered only by crop failures, and other factors which affected their white neighbours as well. Not until the introduction of mechanization of Canadian agriculture did a wide gap between Indian and non-Indian farmer appear. When horses were no longer the centre of farm life, the cultural and educational background of the Indians made it difficult for them to find a place in the new fast-paced technical world.

The tribe went into a slow decline after World War One, being affected both by Canada's depression and the trend towards larger mechanized farms. But World War Two marked a further change in the picture. After the war was over, health services improved, education became better, and the Bloods were encouraged to become masters of their own reserve.

Today, the reserve is run by a chief and council, who direct the work of a large number of Indian employees, including office workers, foremen, and others. The Bloods have their own newspaper, the *Kainai News,* and operate a multi-million dollar factory constructing prefabricated homes. They also have their own supermarket, hospital, recreational buildings and other facilities. Individuals have become successful as nurses, teachers, office workers, carpenters, artists, ranchers and farmers.

Although there are still many problems ahead, the pride of the Bloods has enabled them to become one of the most progressive tribes in Canada.

Each year, the Bloods lined up to receive their $5.00 treaty money. Here, Indian agent Ken Brown gives payments to the tribe in 1958. A short time later, the system was changed so that cheques were sent in the mail.

Women wearing traditional costumes performed the round dance at a gathering in Fort Macleod about 1907.

PEIGAN TRIBE

The Peigan Indians*, who took a reserve west of Fort Macleod after the treaty of 1877, are both the smallest and the largest tribe in the Blackfoot nation. By themselves, they were the smallest Blackfoot tribe to sign treaty in Canada, but when joined with their fellow Peigans in Montana, they form the largest tribe of the nation.

The tribe in Canada is called the *aputoksi-pikuni* or North Peigans, while those in Montana are the *amiskapi-pikuni* or South Peigans. Today, the Canadian group is known simply as the "Peigans" while their southern relatives are officially incorporated as the "Blackfeet Tribe of Montana." One of the earliest references to the groups as separate tribes was made by James Doty in 1855. On Sept. 6th of that year he went to a camp of "about 200 lodges of South Piegans and 80 lodges of North Piegans and Blackfeet." The leader of the North Peigans at that time was Mountain Chief. A U.S. census in 1870 also showed the existence of two tribes, with the North Peigans being under the leadership of Sees Before and North Axe.

In 1874, when the North-West Mounted Police came west, one of the first leaders that Colonel Macleod met was Bull Head, the chief of the North Peigans. According to tradition, his tribe claimed ownership of the area where Fort Macleod was to be built, so the police officer interviewed the chief to gain his permission to build. Bull Head was so impressed with Colonel Macleod that he bestowed his own name upon the officer.

Bull Head died during the winter of 1874-75, and he was succeeded by Sitting on an Eagle Tail, who signed treaty for his tribe. Upon his death in 1885 he was succeeded by his son North Axe.

When the Peigans signed treaty, they asked for a reserve "on the Old Man's River, near the foot of the Porcupine Hills, at a place called Crow's Creek."

This was in one of their favourite wintering areas which had provided a good base from which to hunt buffalo. But even as the treaty was being signed by Sitting on an Eagle Tail, Many Swans, Morning Plume and Crow Eagle, the buffalo were disappearing from their hunting grounds. Commercial hide hunters so reduced the vast herds that they failed to return to Canada in 1879 and the remaining animals were slaughtered in Montana in the following season.

The Peigans who did not pursue the last herds were encouraged to go to their new reserve in 1879, where a farm instructor was appointed to teach them agriculture. By the end of the year about 50 acres of land had been broken and seeded. The Indian Agent reported that a considerable number of Indians had wintered there and their numbers were being daily augmented by small parties returning from the plains.

By the spring of 1880, it was apparent that the Peigans' old way of life had come to an end. The buffalo were gone, the days of wandering were over, and they now had to find new ways of making a living. Canadian Government policy at that time approved the issuing of rations as a temporary measure, but dictated that the Indians become self-supporting as soon as possible. For most reserves, the government was convinced that the Indians should be taught farming regardless of

* *The official spelling in Canada is Peigan while in the U.S. it is Piegan. It is pronounced "pay-gan" (rhymes with "they ran") with the accent on the last syllable.*

Sitting on an Eagle Tail, head chief of the Peigan tribe, at centre, was photographed with other leading chiefs in 1884. Others in the group, left to right, are: front row, Crowfoot, head chief of the Blackfoot, and his foster brother, Three Bulls; back row, Interpreter Jean L'Heureux, Red Crow, head chief of the Bloods, and NWMP sergeant W. Piercy.

the location, fertility of soil or climate. As part of this policy, the decision was made to transform the Peigans into farmers.

The Indians were anxious to find a new source of livelihood and willingly turned to the soil, even though their previous life had been entirely nomadic. Crops of potatoes, turnips, barley and oats were planted, and by the end of 1880 the Agent observed that several onetime warriors were "cross ploughing with their own horses the pieces of land which were broken for them last summer." Indians also went to the nearby Porcupine Hills and brought out timber for log houses to replace their worn tepees.

As part of its treaty obligations, the government issued 198 cows, as well as calves and bulls to the Peigans, but initially these were kept together as a single band herd on the north end of the reserve. Farming was given top priority and the initial results were so encouraging that in 1881 the Inspector of Agencies said,

Potatoes became one of the main crops on the Peigan Reserve during the 1880s and 1890s. Here a group of children pick potatoes at the Anglican mission school.

"These Indians are very well-to-do and will, in my opinion, be the first of the Southern Plain Indians to become self-supporting. They are rich in horses, and having received their stock cattle from the Government, are rich in them too . . ."

The crops were good during the first few years. In 1882, for example, the Agent reported that the Peigans had harvested 2,900 bushels of potatoes, 550 bushels of turnips and 425 bushels of oats, all of which had been sown by Indians. Such men as Big Swan, Towipee, and Takes the Gun Last were very successful in their farming work and potatoes in particular did well. In 1882, the Peigans kept enough for their own needs, sold 50,000 pounds at 2½ cents a pound to the government and another $1,000 worth to nearby settlers. In the following year they supplied seed to the Blackfoot, Sarcee and Stoney reserves.

But by the mid-1880s, their troubles were beginning. Heartened by the success of the potato crops, the government urged the Indians to plant more and more. Then, in 1885 they harvested 6,700 bushels of potatoes but could find a market for only 2,000 pounds. By the end of the year, they were selling 80 pound sacks for as little as 25 cents. Not surprisingly, the Peigans became reluctant to increase the size of their small farms.

Then the few good crop years came to an end. In 1886 a severe drouth left potatoes the size of marbles while an invasion of cutworms added to the problems. All the crops were a complete failure. But this was only the beginning, and over the next fifteen years one crop failure followed another. In 1894 the Agent admitted that "no grain will mature properly in this location, owing to the hot high winds which dry everything up." Yet government policy dictated that the Indians be encouraged to farm, so the work went on. Not until 1898 did the government admit its mistake and its defeat. "Climatic conditions of wind, drought and frost prohibit successful farming on this reserve," stated the Agent. "For about fifteen years a large outlay has been annually made in labour and seed while fruitlessly attempting to grow grain here. While the preparation of the ground was wholesome — though discouraging — occupation for the Indians, the seed grain was literally thrown away, and it is, therefore, the intention of the agency to make no further efforts in that direction but to concentrate all possible attention to cattle-raising."

And so the experiment came to an end. Instead of producing self-sufficient farmers, it had only created disillusionment, frustration and defeat. Many of the Indians who had willingly laboured in the fields now turned more and more to rations as a source of food.

In the meantime, the herd of band cattle had continued to grow, and in the late 1880s, many of the animals were turned over to individual owners. By 1890, there were 141 head owned by individuals, and each year they were permitted to sell a limited number of steers. Also, Indians who wanted to increase the size of their herds could trade their ponies for cattle. By 1894 the herds had grown to 653 head, with 176 ponies being exchanged in that year alone.

The successful introduction of cattle-raising had other favourable effects. Now there was work for other Indians as herders, to cut and haul rail for fences, and to cut and sell hay. For example, in 1889, Takes the Gun Last sold some of his steers and bought a mower and rake. By the end of the year he had filled a contract for supplying 200 tons to a nearby rancher. The enterprising Peigan turned to horse breeding in the following year and bought a fine stallion for $125.

One of the most dramatic success stories of that period was that of Strong Buffalo. By 1895 he had raised a large herd of cattle, and when he learned that the local Anglican missionary was going to England, he decided to accompany him at his own expense. Strong Buffalo knew that England was the home of Queen Victoria, so he wanted to visit her and to air some of the grievances of his people.

In a remarkable letter, written at West Hartlepool, Eng., and published in the *Macleod Gazette* on Feb. 15, 1895, Strong Buffalo told his friends about his adventures. After short visits to Ottawa, Montreal and Halifax, the prairie Indian had put out to sea. "The water came over the boat," he said, "and all the dishes fell off the table and were broken. The big water was as big as from Elk [Red Deer] River in the north to Sheep River in the

The first Catholic mission on the Peigan Reserve shows the primitive conditions under which people lived.

south . . . The ship was very big — there were almost 500 people in it. The ship was as long as from the Mission House to Bear Trail's house."

Once they arrived in England, the missionary took Strong Buffalo to see some of the sights. They went to an iron works where "I saw them pour melted iron like water." He also went to a circus where he saw some amazing things. "I saw white men conjuring. . . I saw a woman lay two eggs. She was only as far as from your house to the kitchen away from me. I saw some elephants; they took a gun and fired with their trunks. I saw a man take his head off and hold it up in his hand, and the head spoke to us."

Strong Buffalo was impressed with England, which he described as being an island as long as from the Red Deer River in Alberta to the Missouri River in Montana. "I have seen houses," he wrote, "one of which would hold all the Bloods, Blackfeet and Peigans."

Finally, he could not help boasting. "If the old Peigan chiefs were to come over the big water," he said, "they would die with fright. When the big ship rolled they would think they were going over, and they would ask the Sun to save them, and then their wives should make a sundance."

Although he saw many strange sights, Strong Buffalo was not able to gain an audience with the queen. When he returned to his reserve, many of his comrades were sceptical about his adventures, particularly his journey over a great ocean. Only when he produced a hand-blown bottle filled with sea water did they accept his tales. Shortly after, efforts were made to elect Strong Buffalo as a chief, but instead he returned to his life as a rancher.

During the early years on the reserve, other events were taking place. An Anglican missionary arrived in 1879, to be the first resident clergyman on any Blackfoot

North Axe became head chief of the Peigan tribe after his father, the former chief, died in 1884.

reserve in Alberta. After he left in 1885, the Peigans were without a permanent missionary until 1887, when a Roman Catholic church and school were opened. An Anglican school was started in the following year and a boarding school in 1890. The Roman Catholics added their own boarding school in 1896. In that year, however, the Agent was not impressed with the progress of the churches and commented that "Little interest is as yet manifested by the Indians in religious matters."

Although the Peigans chose their reserve in 1877, the actual boundaries were not surveyed until 1882 when 181.4 square miles were set aside on the Oldman River, and another 11.5 square miles were reserved as a timber limit in the Porcupine Hills. The size of the reserve was based upon the treaty agreement of five persons per square mile.

In 1877, a total of 589 Peigans were entered on the treaty books, although a number did not attend the ceremonies. In the following year a second census indicated a population of 750. However, an accurate figure was almost impossible to obtain, for the Peigans were always visiting back and forth across the border with their Montana relatives. As a result, many Peigans were listed on the books of both agencies and by 1881 they had inflated their figures to a population of 1,012. Some of these actually were Montana Peigans while others were the result of giving incorrect information about the size of families. As the Peigans were destitute at this time, many had used this ruse in order to obtain larger rations of beef and flour. By 1882, the government had reduced the figure to 849.

During the 1880s and 1890s, the Peigans suffered from many of the white man's diseases, particularly tuberculosis and scrofula. As a result, the mortality rate was high, and the tribe experienced a steady decline in population. In 1896, for example, there were 57 deaths and only 27 births, while in the following year there were 41 deaths and 28 births. By 1898 the population was 536, and it continued to decline to a low ebb of about 250 following the disastrous influenza epidemic of 1918. After that, improved health services and better conditions reversed the trend until by 1986, the reserve had a population of 1,975.

Although farming and ranching were introduced to the Peigan Reserve by the 1890s, life did not change completely from the nomadic days. While they no longer followed the buffalo herds, they did retain their language, religion and customs. The Sun Dance was held, in spite of efforts to suppress it, and each summer most families moved from their log cabins to airy canvas tepees. For example, when a traveller, Walter M'Clintock, visited the reserve at the turn of the century, he found much evidence of the old ways. On arrival, he said, "we looked down upon the broad valley of the North Peigans, through which flowed a river, bordered by huge cottonwood trees . . . While descending towards the valley, we met several young men of the North Peigans, guarding their tribal herds of cattle and horses. They guided us towards the camp of Brings-down-the-Sun."

During his visit in the camp, M'Clintock saw a medicine pipe ritual, children playing in a miniature tepee, gambling games and "the picturesque Indian camp, with its white lodges and brightly blazing outside fires."

Yet changes were taking place. Young children were being taken to the boarding schools where they were taught English, and sometimes learned a trade. In 1899, a railway passed through the centre of the reserve and the siding of Brocket was built within its boundaries. As compensation for the right-of-way, the Peigans received $2,100, with which they built a sawmill. By the end of the first year Indian workers had produced 280,000 feet of lumber, including boards, shiplap, flooring and drop siding.

Events also were moving rapidly outside the reserve. As the surrounding lands were taken up by settlers, people began eyeing the open tracts on the reserve. The Peigans resisted any suggestion that they give up their land, but in 1909 the government forced a vote regarding the sale of the northwest corner of the reserve, and it was approved. A chief, Big Swan, immediately prepared an affidavit claiming that the vote was fraudulent but he was ignored and by the end of the year 28,496 acres of Indian land was sold for $205,681.

By this time, ranching was the main source of income, although new varieties of grain brought a reintroduction of farming. Other Peigans worked for local ranchers or gained work in the district, but the lack of employment opportunities became a chronic problem over the years.

After World War Two, the situation began to change. Health services improved and tuberculosis was virtually eliminated. Educational facilities were upgraded and some young graduates went on to become nurses aides, secretaries, administrators, and welfare workers. The development of the oil industry in southern Alberta, and the construction of related industries in the area for a few years increased the opportunities for work.

Over the years, the Peigans continued to be a quiet, yet independent people, who were not afraid to accept new ideas. They were among the first in Alberta to demand a vote in provincial elections; the first to allow liquor to be brought on their reserve; and the first to assume administration of their own reserve. At the same time, they encouraged the retention of their own culture through Indian Days and other celebrations.

In an attempt to improve their economic situation, they established the Peigan Development Co. to operate a large ranching enterprise, the Pee-Kun-Nee Garment Ltd. to make clothes, while another shop mass produced slipper-type moccasins for sale.

"It is obvious that the people on the Reserve are in the process of change," stated a chief of the tribe. "There are many things in our Indian culture that we wish to preserve that we believe are good. However, if the Peigans are to take their proper place in Canadian society, they must have the courage to change and have the will and belief that change is possible."

The Peigans and other Blackfoot tribes have painted tepees which are rich in symbolism. The lodge at right was known as the horned snake tepee.

SARCEE TRIBE

During the fur trading era, the Sarcees had the reputation of being one of the most warlike and truculent tribes on the Canadian prairies. Loosely allied with the Blackfoot, they were constantly involved in bloody battles and were both respected and feared by all who knew them.

The Sarcees, who today have a reserve on the western outskirts of Calgary, are of Athapascan linguistic stock and are an offshoot of the Beaver Indians of northern Alberta. This separation took place long before the arrival of the fur traders, for in 1772-73 Matthew Cocking referred to them as a distinct tribe of "Equestrian Indians."

Several tales are told among the Sarcees to explain their split with the Beavers, the most common one being that the incident occurred when they were crossing a large lake in mid-winter. As they reached the middle of the lake, a woman noticed an animal's horn protruding from the ice. When she curiously pulled on it, the ice trembled and groaned and suddenly a great crack appeared which cut through the ice, dividing the lake in two. Terrified, part of the tribe rushed north to their hunting grounds while the other fled south. Once separated, those in the southern group kept travelling until they reached the plains where they became known as the Sarcee tribe.

Anthropologists, on the other hand, believe that the Sarcees probably became a distinct band of the Beaver tribe and gradually hunted farther and farther south. In the 1600s, when the Crees pushed westward into their hunting grounds, the Sarcees chose to follow the prairie life while the Beavers drifted north.

The origin of the name "Sarcee" is obscure. Some claim it is a translation of the Blackfoot words *sa* and *ahksi,* meaning "no" and "good"; however, this is not correct, as the proper Blackfoot term for "no

A young Sarcee girl in Calgary about 1887.

good" is *matsokapi,* not *sahksi.* A Sarcee, Pat Grasshopper, claimed his tribe was originally named *Saxsiiwak,* meaning hard or strong people. In their own language they call themselves *tsotli'na,* meaning "earth people"; this refers to the tribe once having been as plentiful as grains of earth or sand.

Bull Head was the head chief of the Sarcees and one of their greatest leaders.

Although they were considered to be Plains Indians by early explorers, the Sarcees spent considerable time in the bushlands and foothills at the edge of the plains. Traders in the late 1700s said they lived near the Rocky Mountains around the headwaters of the North Saskatchewan. In 1810-11, Alexander Henry said they had formerly lived north of the Saskatchewan River and had moved south to Beaver Hills, just south-east of Edmonton.

A good description of the tribe was provided by Henry, who said,

> These people have the reputation of being the bravest tribe in all the plains, who dare face ten times their own numbers, and of this I have had convincing proof during my residence in this country. They are more civilized and more closely attached to us than the Slaves [Blackfoot], and have on several occasions offered to fight the others in our defence. None of their neighbors can injure them with impunity; death is instantly the consequence . . . Most of them have a smattering of the Cree language, which they display in clamorous and discordant strains, without rule or reason. Their own language is so difficult to acquire that none of our people have ever learned it.

During the 1800s, the Sarcees were closely identified with the Blackfoot tribes, particularly the Bloods, and were considered to be part of the Blackfoot confederacy. Whenever they went to trade, they seldom were alone, but usually went with Blood or Peigan parties. A considerable amount of intermarriage took place so that Blood and Blackfoot names became common in the tribe. Yet in spite of this, the Sarcees retained their distinct identity and language, although culturally they were almost identical to the Blackfoot.

As part of the confederacy, the Sarcees drifted farther and farther onto the plains until by the middle of the 19th Century, they were usually found near the Red Deer or Bow Rivers. This remained their favourite hunting ground until they settled on their reserve.

During these fur trading years, the population of the Sarcees fluctuated as this tribe suffered much from the white man's diseases. In the 1780s, after a smallpox epidemic, the population was about 245, rising to an estimated 800 by 1836. Another smallpox epidemic in the following year took a terrible toll, reducing the tribe to about 250 persons. By the late 1860s the population had risen to 420 but another smallpox epidemic in 1869 left them with less than 100 people.

Never again were they a large tribe during the nomadic era. At Treaty No. Seven in 1877 a total of 255 Sarcees were paid and by 1890 there were 280 on their rolls.

At the treaty, the Sarcees were lumped with the Blackfoot and Bloods on a common reserve which bordered the Bow River and extended from a point 20 miles upstream from Blackfoot Crossing all the way down to the Red Deer River. Later, the Sarcee Reserve was officially designated as a strip of land four miles wide "on the south side of the Bow River, commencing three miles above the Blackfoot Crossing and extending as far westerly as may be necessary." It was an arid piece of ground and was entirely unsuitable for agricultural purposes, but at that time the buffalo hunting Sarcees had no thoughts of settling down.

Signing the treaty for the Sarcees was Bull Head, the head chief, and Many Horses, The Drum and Eagle Robe, as minor chiefs. Bull Head, who was to remain the leader until his death in 1911, gained the reputation of being a tough and resiliant warrior.

His strength was effectively proven when the wandering Sarcees were finally obliged to settle down. In 1878 the tribe had found enough buffalo to keep them alive and used Fort Macleod as their headquarters. In the following year, they were persuaded to move to their new reserve, but soon became involved in violent arguments with the Blackfoot. Ang-

This Sarcee camp was pitched on the slopes of Bow River in the 1890s. The town of Calgary can be seen in the background.

rily the Sarcees moved away and many of them followed the last buffalo herds into Montana. In the spring of 1880, the buffalo had all been destroyed and the tribe had to depend upon government rations of beef and flour. They were induced to return to their reserve but the situation still was intolerable. There was constant bickering with the Blackfoot so when the rations ran out, they used this as an excuse to move to Fort Calgary.

Afraid of trouble after the Sarcees tried to burn down a trading post, the three-man Mounted Police detachment at Calgary sent to Fort Macleod for help. "They said they were starving," reported the Indian Agent after going to Calgary and having a council with the Sarcees, "and had determined to remain where they were and die, sooner than return to the Blackfoot Crossing."

The agent told the Sarcees to go south to Fort Macleod where rations were available and although Bull Head still argued in favour of Calgary, at last the Mounted Police pulled down a few of their tepees

and the tribe relented. Their winter trip south was a pitiful one, as described by the constable who took part in this brief so-called "Sarcee war".

"It took some days to get carts, etc., to transport the infirm and very young across the prairie," he said, "and I was put in charge of the whole concern. A troublesome job it was and sometimes the thermometer was 35 below. I was eight days with them, and they took three more to get in after I left them." He had gone ahead because the party ran into a blizzard near the present Stavely. It was too cold to travel, so the Sarcees camped in a coulee for three days. By then the food was almost gone, so the Mounted Policeman set out alone for Fort Macleod for help. Provisions were dispatched immediately and were given to the Sarcees on the way in.

But Bull Head had not changed his mind and by the spring of 1881 officials had grown weary of the problem. "Their dislike to the Blackfoot Crossing," the agent said, "was having their reserve in common with the Blackfeet." Although told that the river would divide them from the other tribe, Bull Head insisted on a reserve "on Fish Creek, eight miles above the supply farm," on the western outskirts of Calgary.

Initially his arguments fell on deaf ears and the tribe was finally prodded into returning to the old reserve with the promise that land would be ploughed for them and ready for seeding. When they got to Blackfoot Crossing, however, the work had not been done. A wise strategist, Bull Head sent a petition to Ottawa outlining the details of his frustrating problems, and three months later an exasperated government gave his tribe the reserve they wanted.

Accordingly, on June 27th, 1883, a new treaty was made with the Sarcees giving them Township 23 in Ranges 2, 3 and 4, west of the 5th meridian "to have and to hold the same unto the use of the said Sarcee Indians forever." This area consisted of 108 square miles, ranging from prairies on the east to deer hunting bushlands to the west. By the end of their first year, 1881, they had built 33 houses to replace their tattered lodges and in the following year they planted their first crops.

The Sarcees were not really interested in farming, but under the watchful eye of their chief a few attempted to plant crops and vegetables. "When work was begun," commented the Indian Agent, "Bull Head turned out, getting his people to work with a will. Quite a number asked to have separate gardens . . ." By 1884 he was able to report that "there are some twelve gardens worked entirely by Indians and containing about an acre each." In the first year, the grain was frozen but they did manage to harvest 30 bushels each of potatoes and turnips. The next year they did a little better harvesting 60 bushels of barley, 35 of potatoes and 70 of turnips.

Living on the outskirts of Calgary had advantages and disadvantages for the Sarcees. During the 1880s and 1890s, when many other Indians were starving, the Sarcees were able to eke out a living by working in the town and surrounding area. They sold wood and hay in town, picked berries, hunted, freighted, sold tanned hides and horses, and worked for local ranchers and farmers. However, with Calgary so close, the tribe also fell prey to bootleggers selling illicit whiskey, and low whites seeking native girls. These were recurring problems and although the Mounted Police and chiefs tried to halt these activities, they became a demoralizing aspect of Sarcee life.

Yet in spite of these problems, the Sarcees clung to their old life. Much of their time was spent hunting, particularly along the mountains, and in the 1890s, many of them wintered in the foothills, far from Calgary's influences.

The government and missionaries tried hard to mold the Sarcees into their own

Two Sarcee women, about 1886.

pattern, but without much success. Although Anglican missionaries came to the reserve in 1886 and opened a school the same year an Agent reported ten years later that there were only three Christians on the entire reserve.

"To understand the difficulties to be contended with in dealing with the Sarcees," he commented, "it must be remembered that they are more tenacious of their customs and superstitions than other Indians ... Until recently they believed themselves doomed to extinction in the near future, and did not appear to wish to exert themselves to avoid what they considered to be their inevitable fate . . ."

The Sarcees had good reason to be discouraged, for life on the reserve seemed to offer nothing but semi-starvation, disease and demoralization. In 1896, for example, there were 12 births and 30 deaths on the reserve, mostly from tuberculosis, scrofula and other diseases. In the following year there were seven births and ten deaths.

However, gradual economic improvements were taking place. In 1896, six men took government cattle on a loan basis and started a budding ranching industry. The Sarcees found ranching to be more like their old buffalo hunting experiences and gradually built up their herds until 1911 they had 304 individually-owned cattle. In 1899, another step towards individual success was achieved when Jim Big Plume, One Spot and Big Crow bought their own mowing machines and went into business for themselves. In 1907 Crow Child became the first self-supporting Indian on the reserve.

These were humble beginnings, yet they indicated that the Sarcees were starting to make the transition to reservation life. By 1900 farming had expanded to the point where 3,723 bushels of wheat and 1,300 bushels of root crops were harvested and 505 tons of hay cut. Many of them continued to sell hay, wood, berries and trees in Calgary, and to join in sports days and other activities. On their reserve, children became accustomed to the schools and adults were more active in their support of the Anglican and Roman Catholic missions.

Located as they are, on the outskirts of a growing city, the Sarcees often were urged to sell their lands. In 1903, they

Cattle are branded in the Indian Agency corral in the 1890s.

40

Active tuberculosis created a serious problem in the Sarcee school. Among this group of students in 1912, two wear bandages to cover open tubercular sores. The boy, standing second left, is David Crowchild, later a chief of the tribe.

leased 11,800 acres for the Sarcee military camp, but the only surrenders which took place were 593.5 acres in 1931 for the Glenmore Reservoir and 940 acres in 1952 for the Department of National Defence. All other pressures to give up the land had been spurned. In 1913, for example, when the head chief Big Belly heard that the City of Calgary wanted Sarcee land, he violently objected "We won't sell our land," he said adamantly. "The white man have all the land; he has taken it from the Indians. All we are left with is one small piece and now he wants it and will leave us with none. I say no, we won't sell."

During the early Twentieth Century, disease was the most serious problem of the tribe. One Indian Department official said that "tuberculosis and trachoma had made such inroads in this band that they were so demoralized and weak that little or nothing was accomplished." In 1920, a doctor who visited the reserve reported that many children in school had active tuberculosis. "All the children except four show the presence of tuberculosis in a state that requires active treatment," he said, "as the children are now fighting a losing battle with this dread disease." As a result of these findings, a medical doctor was appointed Indian Agent and, according to one Sarcee, the reserve became a big sanitorium. The program brought good results and gradually the tribe began to grow from its low population of 160 persons in 1924 to 756 today.

At the same time, there have been many changes. Integrated education was forced upon the tribe in the 1960s but is being countered by attempts to re-establish their own schools. Direct responsibility for band administration has become an initial form of self-government, and a major recreational/cultural complex has been built. The Sarcee Peoples Museum is a showplace, both for the tribe and visitors, while the Indian days/rodeo grounds are popular in summer.

The Sarcees' main foray into economic development has been the creation of Redwood Meadows. This major housing and land development scheme provides for 99-year leases to non-Indians for residential property, a modern golf course, and other facilities. At the same time, the Sarcees continue to resist any ideas of surrendering their land. Instead, they look for new ways to more fully develop their own resources.

STONEY INDIANS

The Stoneys of Alberta are part of a much larger group which had its origins among the mighty Sioux nation. Yet as allies of the Crees, they became violent enemies of the Sioux before beginning their long migration to the slopes of the Canadian Rockies.

Also known as the Assiniboine, their name originated from the term *Assini-pwat,* or Stone People. They separated from the Sioux sometime before 1640 and by 1658 they were mentioned by Jesuit priests as being a distinctive tribe north of Lake Superior. According to tradition, they had been living near the headwaters of the Mississippi when they parted from the Sioux and then went north to ally themselves with the Cree. From there, they drifted westward and within two decades they were in the Lake Winnipeg region.

With the arrival of the British on the shores of Hudson Bay in 1670, the Stoneys were among the first to obtain guns and metal objects. Trader Andrew Graham described them as a powerful nation inhabiting "that extensive track of land to the south and westward of Christianaux Lake [Lake Winnipeg]. They are divided into many tribes and for strength, valour and sound constitution, are not to be surpassed by any other nation."

Equipped with European weapons, the Stoneys and Crees pressed westward along the Saskatchewan River system, driving a wedge between the Gros Ventre and Blackfoot tribes on the south, and the Beavers on the north. Within a short time, some of the scattered bands were hunting all the way to the slopes of the Rocky Mountains, while others pursued the buffalo on the plains of southern Saskatchewan.

Anthony Henday, the first European to visit Alberta, found Stoney bands all along his westward journey in 1754 and when he parted from a group of them near the present town of Innisfail, they went to their own hunting grounds north-west of there.

By this time, there were two main branches of the Assiniboine nation within what is now the Province of Alberta — the Strong Woods, who were a plains people subsisting mainly off the buffalo, and the Swampy Grounds, who lived in the woodland regions.

In 1811, Alexander Henry the Younger described the Stoneys who traded on the North Saskatchewan and hunted on the plains to the south.

> They are generally of moderate stature, rather slender, and very active; there are, however, many tall and well-proportioned men among them. . . . The men adjust their hair in various forms; it is seldom cut, but as it grows is twisted into small locks or tails, about the thickness of a finger. Combs are never used; what loose hair falls out is twisted into those tails, and frequently false hair is added. Many wear numerous tails trailing on the ground; but it is customary to twist this immense flow of hair into a coil on top of the head, broad below and taping above like a sugar loaf nine inches high.

Henry also indicated that the Stoneys were particularly skillful in constructing empoundments for trapping buffalo and were excellent hunters. Also, in paying a left-handed compliment, he said the people, "although the most arrant horse-thieves in the world, are at the same time the most hospitable to strangers who arrive in their camps."

In population, Henry divided the Assiniboines into eleven bands, including the

Stoney Indians chasing wild horses were painted by artist Paul Kane in 1848.

Strong Woods who had 40 tents and hunted on the Battle River, and 30 tents of Swampy Grounds who lived along the Pembina River, north-west of Edmonton. He said that the latter band "never frequent the plains, and are excellent beaver hunters."

During the next several years, hostilities against the Gros Ventres and Blackfoot caused several of the Stoney bands to move farther eastward, while the Strong Woods tended to hunt on the edge of the plains and along the foothills as far south as the Crowsnest Pass. Although often travelling with the Crees, they maintained their own identity and language. While some intermarriage took place, it was never a factor in Stoney identity.

A major change in the life style of the Stoneys occurred in 1840, when a Methodist missionary, Robert T. Rundle, was sent to labour in the region. Working out of Fort Edmonton, he had only limited success with the Blackfoot and Plains Cree, but found many of the Stoneys anxious to hear his teachings. So great was Rundle's impact that leaders such as

Tchakta and Twoyoungmen became his followers. During the next several years, while Christianity had little impact upon other Plains tribes in the area, the Stoneys were embracing the white man's religion. A succession of Methodist missionaries followed Rundle, until in 1873 a permanent mission was built for them at Morleyville, on the Bow River.

By this time, the Stoneys in Alberta had separated into a number of small bands. South, along the foothills to the Crowsnest Pass, the Bearspaw band lived a semiplains existence, and were among the most warlike of the tribe. North of them in the Bow River region were the Chiniki band, who often extended their hunting activities out onto the plains. North of them, near Kootenay Plains and the North Saskatchewan River, the Goodstoney band subsisted almost entirely as a Woodland people.

Beyond the Saskatchewan were two other small Woodland bands which had intermarried to a limited extent with the Crees in the area. These were led by chiefs named Paul and Alexis. A sixth band,

43

descended from the old Strong Woods group, was under the leadership of Sharphead, and hunted in the Pigeon Lake and upper Battle River regions.

Although separated, these bands often camped and hunted together, particularly the Bearspaw, Chiniki and Goodstoney groups. Those under Paul and Alexis remained more isolated, living by hunting and fishing in the bush north-west of Edmonton. Farther south, the Sharphead band usually gravitated to the buffalo-hunting Crees.

Amid such diversity, the common bonds were maintained through language and marriage. In their customs, the Goodstoney, Alexis and Paul's bands tended to be peaceful and dependent upon the white man. The Bearspaw and Sharphead groups, on the other hand, often remained warlike and aloof, while the Chiniki band was a combination of the two extremes.

The Plains-oriented bands usually lived in a state of perpetual warfare with the Blackfoot. When large bands of their enemy were camped on the upper reaches of the Highwood, Bow, or Oldman Rivers, the Stoneys hunted close to the mountains. At the same time, young warriors went out to make regular raids against the Blackfoot, capturing horses and killing their enemies in surprise attacks. Similarly, when the Blackfoot went to trade at Rocky Mountain House or Fort Edmonton, they were harassed by Stoneys and were forced to travel in large numbers to assure themselves any measure of safety.

Those bands which spent much of their time in the mountains and foothills adopted many customs of their Plains neighbours, but usually hunted elk, deer and moose. In the spring and autumn, they usually moved onto the Plains but returned to the woodlands after sufficient numbers of buffalo had been killed. During the remainder of the year, they tra-

Mrs. Job Beaver and Mrs. Peter Wesley follow a traditional custom of the Stoneys by modestly covering their faces while being photographed in 1904.

velled in small bands or family groups as they hunted along the foothills.

In 1873, when the Revs. George and John McDougall established Morleyville mission on the Bow River, it tended to polarize the Goodstoney, Chiniki and Bearspaw bands in that region. Accordingly, when the government called the various tribes together to negotiate Treaty No. Six in 1876, these three bands showed no desire to follow the other members of their tribe — the Sharpheads, Alexis and Paul bands — in joining the ceremonies. This decision was made in spite of the fact that a large part of their territory was north of the Red Deer River. Likely, it was influence of their missionary, who was concentrating his efforts on the Bow River, which caused them to ignore the event.

However, the decision placed the three bands of Stoneys in an awkward situation in 1877 when the last treaty on the prairies was being negotiated, for they were obliged to join with tribes of the hated Blackfoot confederacy to negotiate the terms. In addition, the Stoneys had to travel through enemy territory to Blackfoot Crossing and to camp with their missionary and Hudson's Bay officials on the opposite side of the river from the main treaty group.

They were the only group at the treaty which was under the direct influence of any missionary, and it is likely that Rev. John McDougall dominated both Stoney participation in the negotiations and the decisions of their council. The only chief recorded as having taken an active role was Bearspaw, leader of the most warlike faction, who was under the least control of the missionaries. At the beginning of the discussions, he said:

> We have been watching for you for many moons now, and a long time has gone since I and my children first heard of your coming. Our hearts are not glad to see the Chief of the Great Mother, and to receive flour and meat and anything you may give us. We are all of one mind . . .

At the end of the negotiations, Bearspaw said he was pleased with the treaty, the work of the Mounted Police, and the decision to provide food and treaty money to his tribe.

Signing Treaty Seven on behalf of the 509 members of the three Stoney bands were Bearspaw, Chiniki, and Jacob Goodstoney as head chiefs, while the councillors were James Dixon, Abraham and Patrick Goodstoney, George Twoyoungmen and George Crawler. Through the influence of McDougall, all three bands were centralized on a reserve which was surveyed on Chiniki's hunting grounds in the region surrounding the Morleyville mission.

In the north, the three bands which came under Treaty Six all chose reserves in their traditional hunting areas. Alexis' band, with 42 families, took a reserve on the shores of Lac Ste. Anne, while Paul's band settled on Lake Wabamun. Initially, Sharphead's followers were at Pigeon Lake but when the fisheries failed in 1883, they were induced to take a reserve on Wolf Creek, just south of the present town of Ponoka.

Of all the Stoney bands in Alberta, the Sharpheads had the most tragic history.

A hunting party of Stoneys are seen on White Man's Flats in the Kananaskis valley in 1911.

Stoney Indian children enjoy themselves in the 1930s with a play tepee made of flour sacks.

Although consisting of 36 families in 1883, they were struck down by a measles epidemic three years later and, in 1889 and 1890, epidemics of grippe and influenza reduced them to a mere handful. In the latter year, their reserve was closed, with most of the survivors going to Paul's band, and a few to Morley.

When the Bearspaw, Chiniki and Jacob Goodstoney bands settled on the Stoney Reserve, west of Calgary, the Methodist missionaries had visions of introducing them to an agricultural life. Farming tools were provided and cattle issued, but it took several years for officials to accept the fact that the land was poorly suited for agriculture, and that the Stoneys were hunting people. While the Blackfoot and other neighbouring tribes had been forced to go on reserves after the destruction of the buffalo, the Stoneys could still hunt big game in the foothills. As a result, they were able to continue to kill moose, deer and elk while their Blackfoot enemies had to subsist on rations of beef and flour. As early as 1884, Indian

Agent Magnus Begg told the Stoneys: "the Government considered that they were able to support themselves by hunting and by their increase of cattle, and . . . the rations were cut off from all, with the exception of the widows and infirm."

From the Stoneys' first days on the reserve, the Methodist church played a dominant role in their affairs. A church and school were erected, later followed by a large residential school. Ostensibly, all Stoneys were Christians although traditional practices such as the Thirst Dance and other rites continued to be practised.

As a hunting people, the Stoneys were unwilling to remain constantly on their reserve, the Goodstoney band (later called the Wesley band) often gravitating to the Kootenay Plains, west of Rocky Mountain House, and the Bearspaw band to the headwaters of the Highwood River.

The Stoneys suffered less than other tribes during the starvation decade of 1880s but as more white settlers arrived in the region, pressures were exerted to keep the Indians on their reserve. In particular, criticisms arose during the 1890s about the Stoneys killing game for food, their critics demanding that they conform to all game laws. The Stoneys, on the other hand, claimed that the treaty gave them the right to hunt for food on unoccupied Crown land at any time.

A strong anti-Indian editorial in an 1895 Macleod *Gazette* set the tone for criticisms which continued unabated for the next half century. ". . . the Stoney Indians are wholly responsible for the alarming decrease in big game," it stated. "For many years these Indians have practically been on the hunting path the whole time, and while on the hunt . . . all the active male members of the band take part . . ." The editorial went on to describe their hunting methods and complained that the Indians ignored all game laws.

The scarcity of game in the early 1890s

also forced the Stoneys to hunt across the mountains in British Columbia, but strong criticisms from that quarter resulted in an agreement in 1892 which restricted the tribe to the east slopes of the Rockies. In that same year, Peter Wesley, a leader of the Wesley band, became involved in a dispute with the Indian Agent and took a number of his followers back to their traditional hunting grounds west of Rocky Mountain House. There they remained as squatters until 1947, when the government finally gave them the 5,000-acre Bighorn Reserve in that area.

Similarly, a number of Bearspaw's followers persisted in remaining on the upper waters of Highwood River, even when they were denied government assistance. By the 1940s their plight had become so pitiful that the government finally established the Eden Valley Reserve for them.

While the Stoneys may have started their reservation years with a greater degree of self-sufficiency than the surrounding tribes, this margin was lost during the passing years as hunting and travelling restrictions made it impossible for the people to live off the land. While open and friendly to whites, the Stoneys maintained a strong, introspective unity. The existence of three bands within a single reserve was a constant basis for dispute, particularly as each band elected its own head chief, but at the same time, the tribe was able to retain a distinctive identity.

During the first half of the Twentieth Century, the Stoneys at Morley were subjected to the same type of apathetic treatment common to most reserves. Health services were inadequate, education was in the hands of the church, hunting rights were ignored, and the reserve became intersected by east-west lines of railway tracks, highways, and power lines. Lying on the busy route between Calgary and Banff, the Stoneys suffered many of the inconveniences brought on by the white man's technology but gained few of their benefits.

The Sun Dance remained as one of the most sacred ceremonies of the Stoney Indians, in spite of Methodist influences. This is a view of the Sun Dance lodge in 1926.

One of the most well known figures among the Stoneys was Walking Buffalo, whose registered name was George McLean. He is seen here with his wife at the Banff Indian Days.

After World War Two, however, the Stoneys began to agitate more for their rights. Test cases in court confirmed some of their native hunting rights, while participation in the Indian Association of Alberta brought their problems to the attention of the public.

The Stoney Reserve became one of the first in Alberta to operate its own cultural program during the 1970s, encouraging the use of the Stoney language in school but at the same time introducing university-level courses. The Stoneys opened a wilderness park in 1970, organized annual ecumenical conferences which brought Indians from all parts of the continent, and developed such facilities as craft stores, cafeteria, and service station.

Revenues from gas and oil in the 1970s and 1980s brought a wave of prosperity to the Stoney Reserve, enabling the Wesley band to construct Nakoda Lodge, a major cultural centre. Also, the Indians on this reserve have become more and more active in running their own affairs.

Besides encouraging small businesses on the reserve, it has expanded its ranching operations and has placed emphasis on education as a means of resolving its economic problems.

Similarly, the Stoney reserves west of Edmonton have adapted to their economic situations. Being smaller reserves, they have traditionally had more contact with their non-Indian neighbours and have found regular employment off their reserves. However, improved education and greater involvement in their own affairs have also provided them with more opportunity to choose their own destiny.

The Stoneys of Alberta were able to retain many aspects of their culture during the years when efforts were being made to "Europeanize" them. Now, society has gone a full circle, at last recognizing that the retention of their distinctive culture is one of the tribe's strongest assets.

PLAINS CREE

The Cree are one of the largest tribes in Canada, extending from Hudson Bay to the base of the Rocky Mountains. They are divided into four basic groups, the Plains Cree, Woods Cree, Swampy Cree and Moose Cree. Of these, two of the groups are found in Alberta, the Plains Cree in the central part of the province, and the Woods Cree in the north. The Swampy Cree are mostly in northern Manitoba, while the Moose Cree occupy the area near Moose Factory on Hudson Bay.

The Crees are of Algonkian linguistic stock and each of the four divisions has variations in dialect. Most marked is the use of the letter "y" by the Plains Cree in some words (for example, "I know it," *nikisk-ay-itayn*), where the Woods Cree use "th" *(nikisk-iyth-itayn),* the Swampy Cree an "n" (*nikisk-ayn-itayn*), and the Moose Cree an "I" (*nikisk-ayl-itayn*).

In their own language they were called *Nahiawuk,* sometimes translated as "exact people," while early explorers referred to them as *Kristineaux,* which is based upon an Ojibwa term for the tribe.

The prairie division of the Crees occupied the major part of southern Saskatchewan and much of east-central Alberta in the area of the Battle and North Saskatchewan Rivers. A number of these people spent part of the year in the woodland area north of the Saskatchewan and had a mixed Woodland-Plains culture.

This Plains Cree, Hair in a Knot, was wearing a unique headdress when seen in Calgary about 1884.

The Plains Cree were divided into two main divisions, one on the lower waters of the Saskatchewan and the other near the upper part. The lower group included the Rabbit Skin band, Qu'Appelle People, Touchwood People, and Young Dogs. Those on the upper Saskatchewan were the Willow People, House People, River People, Jackfish Lake People, Frog Lake People, Beaver Hills People, and Rocky Mountain People. Of these, the latter three bands hunted in what is now Alberta.

The buffalo was the basis for their economy. It provided fresh meat for the camps; it was dried and stored; it was pounded, mixed with fat and berries and made into pemmican. The skin provided materials for their lodges, clothing, shields, storage bags, saddles, and numerous other articles, while the paunch, horns and other parts of the body had utilitarian value.

When the buffalo was available, the Plains Cree usually travelled in large bands and used a number of different hunting methods. Sometimes they were hunted on horseback or killed in the deep snow. Most common was the use of the

The buffalo pound was one method used by the Plains Cree while hunting. This sketch was made by Lieut. George Back near Fort Carlton in 1820.

pound which enabled the hunters to kill many buffalo at one time. One such pound was located near a hill eight miles from Hardisty, Alta. "It was built in a natural hollow," said one of the native users, "with the walls of young poplar and willow brush." An entrance to this enclosure consisted of two fences running out for half a mile, gradually widening as they extended from the pound. As the buffalo approached the site, they were stampeded between the two fences, ultimately entering in the corral where they were killed by the hunters.

Other animals eaten by the Cree included deer, moose, elk and antelope, as well as smaller animals, birds and fish. Among the plants used as food were wild turnip, berries and various roots.

The clothing of the Plains Cree was described by trader E. T. Denig in 1855. When speaking of the men, he said,

> While hunting, and indeed at all times through the winter, they wear skin clothing. A coat of buffalo skin with the hair turned inward ties up close to the chin and descends to the knees. The head is covered with a cap of same or rabbit skin, hair inside . . . It is usually ornamented with tufts of skin resembling horns.
>
> The clothing of the women is of the same materials and made in every respect like that of the men except a short frock instead of the skin coat.

The Plains Cree had the reputation of being fierce warriors, with their main enemies being the Blackfoot, Mandan, Sioux and Crow. On occasion they would join with the Ojibwa or the Assiniboine in raiding enemy camps. The Young Dogs were a particularly warlike band made up of both Plains Cree and Assiniboine. In most cases, raids were made for the purpose of capturing horses, although in some instances enemy tribes which encroached on Cree hunting grounds or raided their camps were the object of a revenge attack.

The description of a raid by Little Wolf and a small war party of Crees is typical. They travelled south to the Cutbank

River in Montana where they found a Peigan camp. Most of the good pinto horses were tethered to the tepees, so that night the raiders crept into camp and stole as many as they could. They were not discovered and by morning they were miles away.

When the Peigans learned of the raid, a party went in pursuit but one of the warriors who had a particularly fast horse was killed and scalped as he approached the fleeing Crees. When that happened, the Peigans fell back and the raiders successfully made their way back to their own territory.

In most of these raids, the supernatural was very important, and often a warrior would seek religious powers before going to war. Although there was an all powerful *manitou,* there were also many good and evil spirits which were part of the daily lives of the Cree. The old man stone was a spirit who could help in the buffalo hunt, while the bony spectre, or *pakakos,* could help the good hunter or paralyze an inconsiderate one. There were spirits associated with trees, rocks, animals and birds, as well as the thunder and wind.

The mythical trickster of the Cree was *wisakichak,* who had many adventures which resulted in the making of the earth. In addition, medicine men had great powers in the use of magic and herbs to cure the sick or to destroy an enemy. Among the main ceremonies performed by the Plains Cree were the Thirst Dance, the Smoking Tent, Wetigo Dance and lesser rituals such as the Prairie Chicken Dance, Horse Dance and Medicine Pipe-stem Dance.

Although the western Crees were probably all Woodland people at one time, there is no accurate indication of when they first penetrated the plains. Early Jesuit missionaires and traders who met the Woods or Swampy Cree in Ontario during the 1600s had no knowledge of Plains Cree further west. However, when La Verendrye travelled to Manitoba in 1730, he met the "Cree of the Mountains, Prairies and Rivers," indicating that part of the nation had accepted a prairie life.

A band of Plains Crees was camped at the elbow of the South Saskatchewan when they were photographed in 1872.

This man was among the many Plains Cree in Alberta who settled on reserves near Hobbema and is seen here in the 1890s.

However, the demand for furs and robes by the French traders, and then by the Hudson's Bay Co., accelerated the Cree penetration of the plains. According to the fur trader Andrew Graham, writing in the 1760s, the Crees "in order to search for furs to barter, or because food grew scarce by the large numbers of animals destroyed for their furs and skins . . . has caused them gradually to retire farther inland, until they came amongst the buffalo."

This western penetration was rapid and dramatic. Not only were the Crees anxious to obtain furs, but they became traders themselves, acting as middlemen between the Hudson's Bay Co. and the tribes farther west. Huge profits were made as the Crees exchanged European goods and other objects for valuable furs. In addition, the Crees were now well armed with guns, knives and hatchets, and had little difficulty in occupying the lands of poorly armed enemies.

In their westward move, the Crees drove a wedge up the North Saskatchewan River to the Rocky Mountains, sending tribes retreating to the north and south. The small Sarcee tribe was forced onto the plains, separating from its parent group, the Beavers, who moved northwest to the Peace River area. Similarly, the Blackfoot tribes were pushed back from the North Saskatchewan, and the Gros Ventres withdrew into the present state of Montana.

Often travelling with the Assiniboines, the Plains Cree occupied much of southern Saskatchewan and central Alberta. The more southerly bands adopted a purely plains way of life, while those further north often spent part of their time in the woodlands and part on the prairies.

As the Crees moved west, so did the fur traders, building posts as far west as Rocky Mountain House by 1799. While some of the Plains Crees devoted much of their time to hunting and trapping for the traders, others far out on the plains visited the forts only twice a year.

In addition to the benefits they received from the traders, the Crees were also exposed to alcohol and disease. As early as 1790, one trader observed that "Their unconquerable attachment to spirituous liquors keeps them in endless poverty; for to obtain it they even sell the miserable clothing off their backs." Similarly, smallpox epidemics in 1736 and 1781, wiped out about half the tribe while one in 1818 also caused many deaths. Other diseases like measles and diphtheria killed many more Crees and prevented them from gaining sufficiently in numbers to further expand their hunting grounds.

By the mid-1800s, the Plains Cree had settled into a familiar hunting pattern on the Canadian prairies. They wandered through their territory, following the buffalo, keeping a wary eye open for enemies, and picking winter campsites. Ermineskin, a Cree chief who later settled at Hobbema, said that his band often wintered in the Kootenay Plains, west of Rocky Mountain House. In the spring they followed the buffalo into the Red Deer or Battle River areas and wandered as far east as Battleford. In the summer they drifted west along the Saskatchewan River, reaching Fort Edmonton in time to trade in the fall. Then they wandered south to the Wetaskiwin-Ponoka area before moving towards the foothills for their winter camp.

By 1871, the buffalo were becoming scarce and in that year a number of Plains Cree chiefs appealed to the chief factor at Fort Edmonton for a treaty with the government. "Our country is getting ruined of fur-bearing animals," said Chief Sweetgrass, "and we are poor and want help . . . our country is no longer able to support us. We invite you to come and see us and to speak with us."

In the meantime, the Canadian government was arranging for treaties to be made across the west. The first to affect the Plains Cree was Treaty No. 4, at Qu'Appelle in 1874 which resulted in the surrender of much of southern Saskatchewan. This was signed by such prominent leaders as Loud Voice, Little Black Bear, Flying About, Ready Bow, Day Star and Poorman. The other treaty affecting the tribe was Treaty No. Six, signed in 1876 at Forts Carlton and Pitt. Among the signers were One Arrow, Beardy, Mistawasis, Starblanket, Red Pheasant, Strike him on the Back, Poundmaker, Thunder Companion, and Sweetgrass.

The terms of all western treaties were similar. The Indians gave up their rights

An important religious event of the Plains Cree was the Sun Dance. This view in the 1890s shows ceremonies taking place in the Medicine Lodge.

53

These men represented three of the main Plains Cree reserves in Alberta in the 1920s. They are, left to right, Ermineskin, chief of the Ermineskin band; Charles Rabbit, of the Montana band; and Joe Samson, chief of the Samson band.

to their hunting grounds in return for reserves, treaty money, and assistance in education, farming and health.

None of the treaties affecting the Plains Cree were signed in Alberta, and only a few of the Indians from the area were present. Most prominent of these were Keehiwin and Little Hunter. Most of the others signed later adhesions to the treaty, notably Alexis and Paspaschase at Fort Edmonton in 1877, Bobtail and two councillors at Blackfoot Crossing in 1877, and Puskeakewenin at Sounding Lake in 1878.

By 1880, most of the buffalo had been destroyed and the Plains Cree were obliged to settle on reserves. In Alberta, thirteen reserves were surveyed, but later surrenders and land sales reduced this number to eleven.

The original reserves consisted of Chief Makaoo Reserve, just west of Onion Lake; Onneepow-hayoos and Puskeeah-keeheewin Reserves at Frog Lake; Keehi-win Reserve at Long Lake; Saddle Lake Reserve, jointly occupied by Plains Cree chief Little Hunter and Woods Crees Blue Quill and Pakan; Bear's Ears Reserve, just south of the present town of Waskatenau; Alexander's Reserve at Sandy Lake; Enoch Lapotac Reserve at Winterburn; Paspaschase Reserve, just south of Edmonton; and the Hobbema reserves of Samsom, Ermineskin, Muddy Bull and Bobtail. A few other reserves, such as Alexis, Michel and Goodfish Lake, contained mixtures of Assiniboines, Wood Cree and Plains Cree.

The early years on the reserves were difficult for the Plains Cree. Most of those in Alberta settled in wooded areas where they turned to fishing and big game hunting as a source of food. However, rations had to be issued by the government and early attempts were made to introduce agriculture. So severe were the problems that a number of Plains Cree reserves joined the Riel Rebellion in 1885.

In Alberta, the Frog Lake massacre took place on one of the reserves, while on the Bobtail Reserve near Hobbema, stores were looted.

On the other hand, some Crees refused to be drawn into the fight, and at the Saddle Lake Reserve a messenger of the rebels was killed when he attempted to persuade the Crees there to join.

But the rebellion affected everyone and, when it was over, the Crees lived in the shadow of its defeat for several generations.

By the 1890s, most of the people subsisted through a combination of hunting, fishing, farming, rations and working for neighbouring white men. There were some exceptions, such as Little Hunter's son who in 1889 owned his own haying outfit and was doing contract work. But most of the Crees lived only part of the year in their tiny log cabins and spent the rest of the time hunting and fishing.

The missionaries had been among the Crees since the 1820s, often accompanying them on buffalo hunts. In 1865, Father Lacombe had attempted to start an agricultural colony for the Plains Cree near the present village of Brosseau, but he had been unsuccessful. As long as there were buffalo on the plains, the Crees had no interest in farming.

After the Indians settled on their reserves, they were soon joined by Methodist and Roman Catholic missionaries. Churches and day schools were built, to be followed by larger residential schools at Saddle Lake, Edmonton, and Hobbema. In addition, a large industrial school for Crees was built at Red Deer by the Methodists, and a number of Cree students were sent to the Oblate industrial school near High River.

During these years, the population of the reserves showed a steady decline. For example, the Keehiwin band had 211

Plains Cree Indians from the Hobbema Agency perform a dance in Wetaskiwin in 1898.

members in 1876, but the population had dropped to 145 by 1908. In later years, however, with the improvement of health services the trend was reversed and by 1983 the reserve had a population of 859.

By the turn of the century, the declining population resulted in pressures to surrender parts of their reserves to white settlers. In the 1890s, the Paspaschase Reserve was surrendered and is now part of Edmonton; similarly, the Bear's Ears Reserve was closed. In addition, large sections of land were sold from such reserves as Enoch's, Saddle Lake, Bobtail, Samson, and Muddy Bull.

Although many school graduates became successful farmers and ranchers during the 1920s and 1930s, the problems of health and education were often too great to overcome. A number of native attempts to solve these problems resulted in the formation of the League of Indians of Alberta in 1933, and the Indian Association of Alberta in 1939. However, not until after the Second World War did the Crees have an opportunity to develop. In addition, the discovery of oil on the Enoch Reserve and at Hobbema resulted in more band funds being available for local improvement.

As a result of better educational services, many Plains Crees have become teachers, nurses, administrators and band employees. Others have been involved in the publication of a newspaper, radio broadcasting, and other modern services, while on some reserves, farming, fishing and cattle raising have continued to be basic industries.

Plains Cree and Agency staff students at the mission school at Hobbema were photographed in the 1890s. Left to right, standing: Mabel German, Sophia Baptiste, Georgina Potts, Clem German (child), Maggie Twins, teacher Hanna Shaw, and Howard German; sitting: Abbie Louis, Joseph Twins, Emma Potts, John Louis, James Ward, Lazarus Potts, and Maria Souzi. The dog was named Dot.

WOODLAND CREE

The Woodland Cree were one of the most extensive and widespread tribes of Canada, their hunting grounds in the Nineteenth Century ranging from Hudson Bay to the Rocky Mountains, and from the plains to the sub-Arctic. Often sharing their areas with the Ojibwa and Assiniboine, they were hunters and trappers who were the mainstay of the fur trade.

The Woodland Cree were among the first tribes to meet British traders on Hudson Bay in the 1600s. At that time their native hunting grounds extended only as far west as the present Alberta-Saskatchewan boundary, with the Beaver Indians inhabiting northern Alberta.

The Crees soon profited from the knives, guns and utensils which were available from the traders in exchange for furs. Not only did they begin to concentrate on trapping, but they also became middlemen, trading the metal objects to tribes farther west.

Within a few years, the hunting area of the Woodland Cree was being heavily trapped, so the tribe began to push south and west. A fur trader, Andrew Graham, writing in the late 1700s, observed:

> Either to avoid Europeans, or in order to search for furs to barter, or because food grew scarce by the large numbers of animals destroyed for their furs and skins, one or more of these reasons has caused them gradually to retire farther inland . . .

Others remained close to the traders, living both by trapping and by providing fresh meat to the posts. These people were known as the "Home Guard" Indians, while those farther away were called Southard Indians (because their hunting grounds were southward from Hudson Bay.) "The nation is very numerous and divided into many tribes," said Graham. "A very small portion come down to trade at York and Churchill settlements . . . With [their] skins they come down annually to the settlements, and as only so

small a number as two hundred small canoes undertake the voyage, the others who remain inland send their goods with any of their acquaintance."

Within a short time, the Woodland Cree had pushed the Beaver Indians back to the upper waters of Peace River and occupied much of the central and northern portion of Alberta. By the early 1800s, the Woodland Cree were in control of the vast forest belt of the Canadian west and were following the traders into the more northerly regions.

During their period of recorded history, the fate of the Woodland Cree was closely intertwined with the fur traders. Their annual wanderings centred upon the forts and by the early 1800s many had abandoned important aspects of their own culture and dress in favour of European ways. Many fur traders married Woodland Cree women and a group known as Metis or half-breed came into being. Some Metis were hunters and trappers like their mother's people, but others received a good education and entered the service of the Hudson's Bay or North West Company as clerks or traders. Such surnames as Cardinal, Pelletier, Cunningham, McGillis, Martel and Sutherland became common among the native population.

The Woodland Cree lived primarily off the moose, deer, elk, smaller animals and fish. As the animals tended to travel singly or in small herds, the Indians, too, remained in small groups. Often they remained in family units, meeting other

The interior of a Woodland Cree tepee was sketched in 1820 by explorer Robert Hood.

members of the tribe only for ceremonies or visits to the trading posts. Unlike their brothers on the Plains, who travelled in large bands, the woodland people did not maintain a strong tribal identity, nor did they develop a complex structure of societies and religious fraternities which were so common to the plains.

But perhaps even more than the Plains Cree, the woodland people were deeply religious. Because families lived lonely and isolated lives, they were keenly aware of the fine line between survival and starvation. If the moose could not be found; if the rabbit population reached its low cycle; or it winter storms kept the people huddled in their lodges, their scanty food supply could quickly run out. For that reason, supernatural help was important to the Woodland Cree; the forests were filled with evil spirits which could kill, maim or deform the luckless hunter. One of these spirits was the Witigo, a great cannibal monster with a heart of ice which roamed the woods and fed upon the unwary. A spirit of the Witigo could also enter the body of a person, turning him into a cannibal who had to be killed by his relatives.

Another spirit of the forest was the Pakakos, which was a skeleton spectre which could fly through the air and attack a hunter. The Cree believed that this spectre preyed upon poor hunters — men who wounded animals and let them escape or killed unnecessarily. When the Pakakos attacked such men, it could paralyze their arms or otherwise make them incapable of further hunting.

There were also sorcerers among the Woodland Cree. These men were believed to have had supernatural powers by which they could kill an enemy, make a woman fall in love or drive a man insane. Similarly, these sorcerers could provide amulets which could offset the evil influences of other supernatural forces. According to one authority, the Plains Cree looked down upon their woodland relatives because they were poor fighters "but also feared them for their magical prowess."

From the evidence of early travellers, it is apparent that while the woodland people were not often involved in warfare, they were gallant fighters. Incidents of battles with the Beaver and other enemy tribes during their westward penetration indicates that they were as capable as their plains relatives. For example, explorer Alexander Mackenzie in 1801 said that the Crees "had driven away the natives of the Saskatchiwine and Missinipy Rivers . . . from there they proceeded West by the Slave Lake . . . on their war excursions, which they often repeated, even till the Beaver Indians had procured arms, which was in the year 1782."

But the pursuit of food was the main occupation of the Woodland Cree. Fish were caught in nets during the winter, with the women often performing this work. On other occasions fish were speared by the men, gathered in traps, or caught with hooks made of eagle claws.

Smaller animals and birds like rabbits and partridges were snared with sinew; ducks and geese were lured with decoys and shot; young birds were caught in snares hidden in shallow water. Larger animals such as moose and deer were shot with bows and arrows, often being killed from canoes while swimming across rivers or lakes.

In trapping, the Woodland Cree used snares, deadfalls and wooden traps. Beaver and muskrat were often dug out of their lodges.

When discussing their costumes, a traveller in 1819 said,

Their cloathing is made of leather and cloth. The dress of the men is composed of the following articles. A cloth or bandage is

A Cree woman uses an earthern fireplace for cooking and heating her log cabin in the Lesser Slave Lake area. Note the three copper trade kettles.

passed between the legs and fastened to the waist at each extremity. The leggins extend to the hips and are also attached to the waist. If made of cloth they are bound with various colours on the outside seams and bottom, but if of leather the seams are fringed by cutting the border into strips. A long waistcoat is worn, tied or buttoned in front, and over it, a frock, which cover the thighs, furnished with a hood above and tied around the waist with a belt. The cap is an otter or marten skin decked with the feathers of an eagle's tail. In winter, they carry a blanket over the shoulders which is their only bedding when hunting.

The stockings of the women are gathered at the knees, and ornamented at the ankles with rows of beads. An under garment covers the body from the neck to the feet, the sleeves not being sewed to it, but attached to one another by a strip of cloth across the back. Their hoods are fastened at the neck, forming a tippet on the shoulders which, as well as the breast of the under garment, is adorned by stained porcupine quills, beads and tassels of leather.

In these costumes, the women were considered very attractive. Alexander Mackenzie noted that, "Of all the nations which I have seen on this continent, the Knisteneaux [Cree] women are the most comely. Their figure is generally well proportioned, and the regularity of their features would be acknowledged by the more civilized people of Europe."

There was a clear division of duties between the men and the women. The latter did all the cooking, tanning hides, making clothing, quillworking and beading, cutting firewood, making snowshoes, hauling sledges, pitching lodges, and helping with snaring game and net fishing.

The men were responsible for hunting, fishing, making canoes and sledges, trapping, making objects of religion and war, and protecting the camp.

Because of the marginal life of the Woodland Cree, where starvation was always a threat, the arrival of the fur traders brought many benefits. The gun soon replaced the bow and arrow in hunting; sinew or rawhide nets were abandoned in favor of European ones; and the availability of knives, metal pots, axes and other utensils made life much easier. Similarly, the tedious task of tanning hides was sometimes eased when shirts, blankets and other cloth objects were bought.

But the presence of white traders also created serious problems. The woodland people abandoned their previous life cycle, which consisted of moving about within their hunting grounds in a constant search for food. Now the emphasis was placed on trapping and some of the animals which provided both pelts and meat were slaughtered indiscriminately. When they were in short supply, the Crees either moved farther away or eked out an existence near the trading posts.

For example, in the late 1700s, a trader described the cycle of Indians living near his fort. In the fall, they were given supplies on credit and went out trapping in the bush. In the spring they returned with their furs, settled their accounts and bought more supplies or liquor from any money still remaining. In May they went out goose hunting for the fort, while others hunted big game or acted as messengers.

A standard payment for summer work at that time was two quarts of brandy for a deer. To earn a quart of brandy a man had to bring in either ten deer tongues, ten fish, one porcupine, one beaver, or six pounds of deer fat or to get a pound of powder and shot he had to kill 20 geese.

Because many of the Indians became dependant upon the trading posts for survival, they tended to be more influenced by European practises than the Plains tribes to the south. This meant the abandoning of religious practices, costumes and beliefs.

More immediate problems, however, were the introduction of liquor and disease. Even as early as the 1770s Andrew Graham wrote, "They are so addicted to drunkenness that they practise every art

A Woodland Cree woman in northern Alberta stretches a moose skin on a wooden frame as the first step in a tanning process.

to procure brandy, and had they free access to it, death only would put an end to their debauch, of which we have had instances." Similarly, he noted that tuberculosis, measles, smallpox and other diseases introduced by the Europeans, resulted in a high mortality rate.

The fur traders moved into northern Alberta in the 1780s in the wake of the westward moving Cree. By 1800, the Woodland Cree were being served by trading posts on the North Saskatchewan as well as on the Athabasca and Peace Rivers and at Lesser Slave Lake.

By the middle of the 19th Century, missionaries began to visit the Woodland Cree in northern Alberta, and later established missions among them. The first was a Catholic priest, Father Jean B. Thibault, who came up the Saskatchewan River in 1842 and spent some months among the Plains and Woodland Cree at Frog Lake. In the following year he settled at Lac Ste. Anne, from which

point he worked primarily among the Metis. In 1845 he went to Cold Lake, while in the same year, Father Joseph Bourassa opened a mission at Lesser Slave Lake.

As early as the 1840s, Methodist missionary Robert Rundle had visited the Woodland Cree, but he devoted most of his energies to the Plains people. In 1855, the Rev. Henry B. Steinhauer, an Ojibwa Indian, settled at Lac La Biche, later moving to Whitefish Lake, where he also worked with the Cree.

The third denomination in the area was the Anglican Church. Bishop W. C. Bompas served in the Mackenzie River area in the 1850s, and began to visit the Woodland Cree and Beavers at Fort Vermilion in 1868. Finally, in the mid-1870s, Rev. Alfred Garrioch opened a permanent mission at that place.

In the latter part of the century, the Anglicans were the main denomination in north-western Alberta, with the Methodists dominating the Saddle Lake region, and the Catholics the areas north-west of Edmonton and in the Fort Chipewyan region. In many cases, native people were employed as catechists or lay-readers, and soon Christianity had a strong influence in all communities.

In the 1880s and 1890s, residential schools were opened at such points as St. Albert, Fort Vermilion, Lesser Slave Lake and Fort Chipewyan. In part, the missionaries found it easier to teach the children when they were together in one place; but equally important was a desire to take them away from their families to offset practises which the missionaries considered "pagan".

By the 1890s, most Woodland Cree bands were well mixed with Metis, and the influence of the Hudson's Bay post manager and local missionary were unquestioned. The big change in this routine occurred in 1898, immediately following the discovery of gold in the Klondike. Many gold seekers went to the Yukon via northern Alberta, and still others were attracted to the territory and remained to trap, trade or farm. This immediately affected the power of the Hudson's Bay Co. and caused a breakdown of their credit system. It also caused a great uneasiness among the Woodland Cree leaders, who feared that their lands would be taken from them by the new settlers.

The Crees farther south had signed Treaty No. Six in 1876, and although some Woodland Crees in the Saddle Lake region had been affected, most of those father north were not. Accordingly, in 1899, the Canadian Government sent two expeditions into northern Alberta. If a person considered himself to be an Indian, he could accept Treaty No. Eight from the Treaty Commission and retain his status. On the other hand, if he was a Metis or half-breed, he could be regis-

A large mudded log house became a comfortable winter replacement for a tepee among the Woodland Cree. In summer, however, they still returned to their tents.

tered by the Scrip Commission and receive a paper which entitled him to 160 acres of land.

Some of the Indians were suspicious about the treaty. Keenooshayo, for example, said:

> Do you not allow the Indians to make their own conditions, so that they may benefit as much as possible? Why I say this is that we to-day make arrangements that are to last as long as the sun shines and the water runs.

However, they agreed to the terms, with Mootoos and Keenooshayo being among the first to sign at Lesser Slave Lake. From there the commissioners went down the Peace River and up the Athabasca, gaining the signatures of other leaders.

Attempts were made, both in the Treaty Six and Treaty Eight areas, to encourage farming. Initially, however, they met with little success. For example, in 1881 the Indian Agent reported on conditions At Lac La Biche. "The Indians had no grain and potatoes that they could rely upon for seed this year," he said, "and owing to the want of time and ammunition, had the prospect of a bad winter." Similarly in 1890, when reporting the progress of the Wah-sat-an-ow band, he said, "Their farming operations are on such a small scale that it is little more than a name. A few of them, however, try to put in a small crop, and the majority hunt or fish as the fancy takes them."

In fact, many of the Woodland Cree saw little need to farm. As long as they could live by hunting, trapping and fishing, they preferred to do so. Although there were exceptions, this situation continued well into the Twentieth Century, until the decline of fur prices and fur bearing animals, as well as restrictions on commercial fishing, made it impossible for the old ways to continue.

In the meantime, many Indians received an education in residential schools, or later in integrated schools, and began

One of the important Woodland Cree leaders to sign Treaty No. Eight in 1899 was Moostoos, seated at left. The Mounted Policeman is Sgt. K. J. Anderson.

to enter other areas of labour. Some became bush workers, loggers, oil field workers and hunting guides. Others went to the major cities where they became office workers, secretaries, nurses aides and teacher aides.

Within the past two decades, many Woodland Cree have been involved in band management, nursing, teaching, and professions, while on the reserves, farming, commercial fishing, trapping and hunting have continued to be important sources of livelihood. With their close association with the white man for so many years, the Woodland Cree have been better prepared than many tribes to meet the demands of today's society.

CHIPEWYAN INDIANS

Inhabiting a desolate land, where survival often depended upon the unpredictable movements of the caribou, the Chipewyan Indians were a hardy people who learned to survive under extreme conditions.

They are part of the Athapascan linquistic group, as are their neighbours, the Beaver, Slavey, Yellowknife, and Dogrib tribes. Their name Chipewyan was taken from the Cree term "pointed skins," given to them because of their practise of having tail-like protrubances hanging from the bottom of their shirts. In fact, this characteristic gave rise to a fantastic story of a race of part-human, part-animal creatures which inhabited the far north. The confusion arose from the difficulties of early interpreters in explaining that the tails belonged to the shirts, not to the men. The Chipewyans also were known as *Wechepowuck* by the Crees, Montagnais by the French, and Northern, or Northard Indians by the British.

At the time of white contact about 1700, the Chipewyans hunted in the area between Great Slave Lake and Hudson Bay. To the north were their deadly enemies, the Inuit, while south were the Cree, and west the Slavey and Dogrib. And although their area extended to the shores of Hudson Bay, they were not a sea-going people but usually remained in the interior.

Henry Kelsey, a Hudson's Bay Co. fur trader, learned of their existence in 1689 and tried to bring them to the coast to trade, but was unsuccessful. In 1716, however, William Stewart succeeded in locating them and brought ten of them to York Factory to trade. A year later, Fort Churchill was established on Hudson Bay, at the south-east edge of their hunting grounds, and soon the Chipewyan were visiting the post on a regular basis. Those who hunted in the eastern part of their land came each spring and autumn, while those farther away visited only once in every three years.

When the Chipewyans traded, they limited their purchases to guns, ammunition, and metal utensils and soon opened their own thriving intertribal trade with the Dogribs and other interior tribes. In addition, guns gave them superiority in the war which enabled them to push northward into Inuit territory, and westward to the Peace River. In 1778, when a North West Co. post was opened on Lake Athabasca, most of the Chipewyans abandoned the long trek to Hudson Bay. When a chief arrived at the newly-opened post in that year he said he was "pleased at having Goods at the Lake and promised to stop all his people from going to Churchill."

In the meantime, the Crees farther south had also received arms from the traders on Hudson Bay and had pushed westward along the North Saskatchewan River. When the Beaver Indians retreated from what is now north-eastern Alberta, the area was occupied by Woodland Cree from the east and Chipewyans from the north. The latter tribe often penetrated as far south as Beaver Lake during its hunting expeditions. By the time the tribes had carved out their new areas, the Chipewyans were in firm control of the lower waters of the Peace and Athabasca Rivers, Lake Athabasca, and their old hunting area to the east.

Explorer Alexander Mackenzie in 1793 described the Chipewyans as "sober, timorous, and vagrant, with a selfish disposition which has created suspicions of their

Portrait of Nasurethur, a Chipewyan Indian, about 1926.

integrity." At the same time he found them easy to approach and willing to share their knowledge of the land with the explorer.

He described them as not tall, but seldom corpulent, with a darker complexion than other tribes and with deep piercing eyes. Some of the men wore black bushy beards, although the majority plucked out any facial hairs.

The Chipewyans had the reputation of being fierce warriors who were frequently fighting their neighbours. In 1771, for example, Samuel Hearne engaged some Chipewyans at Fort Churchill to assist him in finding the Coppermine River. When between seventy and eighty warrior accompanied him, he learned that the trip was an excuse for attacking the Inuit. When they finally discovered a small encampment, the Chipewyans made an early morning attack and slaughtered thirty men, women and children.

"The shrieks and the groans of the poor expiring souls were truly horrible," said Hearne, "and was much increased at the sight of one young girl, about eighteen years old, whom they killed so nigh me, that when the first spear struck her, she fell down and twisted about my feet and legs."

In about 1760, the Chipewyans established an uneasy peace with the Crees after they had driven them away from Lake Athabasca. Similarly, they fought with the Yellowknife and Dogrib Indians to prevent them from opening direct trading relations with the forts on Hudson Bay, but once the companies moved inland, the need for hostilities ceased. With the Inuit, however, the feeling of hatred was retained and occasional skirmishes continued well into the Nineteenth Century.

The caribou was the main source of food for the Chipewyans. During the summer, one of the favourite means of killing them was by spearing them from canoes as they swam across rivers or lakes. On other occasions they were driven into traps where they were killed with arrows. In winter they were snared or caught in deep snow.

Other animals, such as buffalo, muskox, and moose were killed in lesser numbers, while fish and waterfowl often supplemented the Chipewyans' meagre diet. As their hunting grounds included both the open barrenlands and woodlands farther south, the bands often moved from place to place, either following the migrations of the caribou or eking out a marginal existence.

Unlike the tribes to the south, the Chipewyans did not have any structured form of leadership, other than the head of a family. As the people usually travelled in family groups, this was sufficient, except during intratribal disputes, when superior strength often dictated the outcome.

Similarly, the Chipewyans had only a form of guardian spirit worship as their religion. There were no public prayers nor rituals; instead, each individual had his own spiritual protector, sometimes as the result of a dream. Often the figure of this protector was painted on a shield when going to war or the skin of the animal was buried with a man when he died.

On the other hand, great faith was placed in the abilities of Indian doctors who, through the use of medicinal herbs and incantations, could effect cures for various ailments. These men, whose powers often came as a result of visions, could also cast evil spells upon their enemies.

The winter dress of a Chipewyan man consisted of a thigh-length caribou skin shirt with the hair left on; moccasins attached to leggings which extended to the waist where they were supported by a belt; and a breechcloth which hung down in front and back. In severe weather, the moccasins were stuffed with caribou or moose hair. The man also wore a belt, mittens and a cap made from the skin of a deer's head. Over this entire costume he wore a robe made of several caribou or fawn skins sewn together.

"Thus arrayed," said Alexander Mackenzie, "a Chepewyan will lay himself down on the ice in the middle of a lake, and repose in comfort; though he will sometimes find a difficulty in the morning to disencumber himself from the snow drifted on him during the night."

The woman's costume consisted of a dress which extended to her ankles and was fastened at the waist with a belt. For those with children, the dress was very full about the shoulders so that the infants could be carried on their backs next to the skin. On their legs, the women had moccasins and leggings which were tied below the knee.

Those who visited the Chipewyans during the Eighteenth Century felt that the place of the woman was inferior to that of other tribes. She was the beast of burden who carried the family posses-

Two Chipewyan women are seen picking berries north of Lake Athabasca shortly after the turn of the century.

66

sions or pulled the toboggan; the men had the reputation for beating their wives unmercifully. Yet when William Butler visited a Chipewyan camp on the Athabasca River in 1873, he found a pleasant family scene.

> Some ten or twelve people congregated around a bright fire burning in the centre. The lodge was large, requiring a dozen moose skins in its construction. Quantities of moose or buffalo meat, cut into slices, hung to dry in the upper smoke. The inevitable puppy dog playing with a stick; the fat, greasy child pinching the puppy dog, drinking on all fours out of a tin pan, or sawing away at a bit of meat; and the women, old or young, cooking or nursing . . .

Because of their marginal life, the Chipewyans had a culture which was easily replaced by practises brought in by Cree employees of the fur trade. As a result, outside rituals were introduced, and even the more simple art forms were abandoned in favour of ornate designs borrowed from neighbouring tribes. Similarly, objects of European manufacture soon replaced their own.

But a more disastrous effect of the white man's arrival was the introduction of diseases. An epidemic of smallpox in 1781 wiped out nine-tenths of the tribe, in some cases taking away entire bands. Partly as a result of this catastrophe, the Chipewyans ceased their warring activities against enemy tribes. The population of the tribe at the time of white contact was estimated to be 3,500 but it declined to less than 1,000 at the beginning of the Twentieth Century because of disease and starvation.

During the early period, the Chipewyans refused to accept alcohol. In the 1780s, Andrew Graham commented that they "drink no spiritous liquors," while in 1793 Alexander Mackenzie said that "As the people are not addicted to spiritous liquors, they have a regular and uninterrupted use of their own interest." Yet the liquor continued to flow into the trad-

ing posts and by 1819 the situation had so changed that a traveller noted that "They are as much corrupted by spiritous liquors as the Crees."

Soon the entire economy of the Chipewyans became tied to the trading posts. The tribe depended upon them for essential goods and devoted much of their time to trapping and preparing hides for the trade.

During the mid-Nineteenth Century, missionaries began to visit the Chipewyans and found ready converts among them. Among the first was Father Joseph Bourassa, who went among the Chipewyans and Crees at Cold Lake in 1845. In 1865, Bishop W. C. Bompas of the Anglican Church began his work in the Mackenzie River area, and later extended his services to the tribes farther south. Soon both the Roman Catholics and Anglicans had established churches in Fort Chipewyan and in 1899 a visitor to the fort reported that "All the Indians we met were with rare exceptions professing Christians, and showed evidences of the work which missionaries have carried on among them for many years. A few of them have had their children avail themselves of the advantages afforded by boarding schools established at different missions."

During the latter part of the Nineteenth Century, one band of Chipewyans normally hunted in the Cold Lake area, near the North Saskatchewan, while the others ranged much farther to the north. In 1876, when the Canadian government negotiated a treaty with the Cree and Ojibwa Indians, the southern leader of the Chipewyans, Kin-oo-say-oo, and his head man, Antoine Xavier, attended the sessions at Fort Pitt and signed on behalf of their followers.

Not until 1899 did others in the tribe discuss a treaty. In that year, the Chipewyans in northern Alberta, Northwest Territories and part of northern Saskat-

Tepees and tents were pitched on the rocky ground surrounding Fort Chipewyan.

chewan signed Treaty No. 8 with the government. Signing for the Chipewyans were Laurent Dzieddin and Toussaint, of Fond du Lac; Alex Laviolette, Julien Ratfat and Sept. Heezell, of Fort Chipewyan; Michael Mamdrille and William Kiscorray, of Fort Smith; Adam Boucher, of Fort McMurray; and Louison Ahthay, Oliver Ajjericon, Vital Lamoelle, and Paulette Chandelle, of Great Slave Lake. A total of 215 Chipewyans accepted the terms of the treaty during the long trek made by the Commissioners through the north.

The treaty provided for the surrender of all hunting grounds by the Indians in exchange for reserves, treaty money, tools and implements, and other benefits.

The Chipewyans had doubts about the terms which were offered. "The Chief at Fort Chipewyan," said the commissioner, "displayed considerable keenness of intellect and much practical sense in pressing the claims of his band. They all wanted as liberal, if not more liberal terms, than were granted to the Indians of the plains."

At last, however, they accepted the treaty. In 1907, the remainder of the Chipewyans in northern Saskatchewan signed Treaty No. 10, receiving the same terms.

For some years, after these events, life went on as before, the only exception being that each spring, an Indian Agent travelled through the area paying treaty money. For example, when describing the trip in 1908, the agent said: "We proceeded on the Hudson's Bay Company steamer *Primrose* to Fort Chipewyan . . . On June 25th we paid annuities to the 564 Indians in the two bands there. During the year 25 births and 14 deaths occurred." Describing conditions in that year, he said, "They reported a hard winter and a shortage of fur, but they managed to survive the winter with but little assistance from the trading posts."

In Alberta, five reserves were established for the Chipewyans. The largest of these was the southerly Cold Lake Reserve which, by 1983, had a population of 1,045 persons. Adjoining Lake Athabasca was the Chipewyan Reserve with a population of 315 while north of Lac la Biche was the Janvier Reserve with 265 people and the McKay Reserve with 226. A reserve at Fort McMurray contained mixed Chipewyan and Cree bands totalling 140 persons. In addition, six reserves were surveyed in Saskatchewan and two in Manitoba, while the Indians in the Northwest Territories did not receive reserves.

For the Indians in the north, the dramatic change in their lives occurred during the 1920s when aviation ended the isolation. Within a few years, lakes were being fished commercially and the products flown out to eastern markets; men were travelling to their distant traplines by airplane; and outside civilization was thrust upon them. Similarly, the decline of fur markets after the Second World War, the loss of trapping areas, the improvement of educational facilities, and the expansion of welfare services all had dramatic but not always positive effect upon the tribe. Yet many Chipewyans have prospered, some seeking new opportunities in urban communities and others finding a satisfactory life on their reserves.

A Chipewyan family was photographed in front of their home at Heart Lake about 1924.

These three Chipewyan chiefs signed Treaty No. Eight on behalf of their tribe in 1899. Left to right are Laurent Dzieddin, the chief Maurice Piche, and Toussaint.

Chipewyans gathered in 1911 for their treaty payments at Portage La Loche.

70

BEAVER INDIANS

Inhabiting the upper waters of the Peace River, the Beaver Indians were known to early fur traders as excellent moose hunters and trappers. Independent and more warlike than their neighbouring Chipewyan cousins, they tried to protect their lands from incursions by the Crees, and at the same time fight the weaker Senaki Indians to the west.

The Beavers are of Athapaskan linguistic stock, their language being closely related to that of the Chipewyan and Slavey, as well as the prairie Sarcees, who broke away from the Beavers before the arrival of Europeans. The Beavers were known as *Tsattine,* or "dwellers among the beavers," which apparently was based upon the name *Tsades,* or "river of beavers," the native term for peace River.

During the period of recorded history, the Beavers hunted in the area along the Peace River from Fort Vermilion to the Rocky Mountains. Although at one time there were at least five different bands, disease had reduced these to three by the latter part of the Nineteenth Century. One band which hunted in the region of Fort St. John and northward to Liard River was also known to early travellers as the Rocky Mountain Indians. Another band traded at Fort Dunvegan and hunted northward as far as the Hay River, while the third band traded at Fort Vermilion and hunted in that area.

Earlier, a four band had existed near Peace River town, but when the population was reduced through disease, the survivors joined the Fort Dunvegan group. A fifth band was said to have existed near Lesser Slave Lake about the time of first European contact, but they were probably wiped out by smallpox.

According to explorer Alexander Mackenzie, the Beaver Indians originally inhabited a vast area bounded roughly by the Alberta-Saskatchewan border on the east; Peace River on the north; Peace River town on the west; and Lesser Slave Lake to the south. Immediately south of them were the Sarcees, whose lands extended to the North Saskatchewan River.

After the Crees obtained guns from European traders in the early 1700s, they began to move westward, driving the Beavers before them. Bands of Crees travelling along the Churchill River system and others moving up the Saskatchewan eventually joined together near Beaver Lake, on the Alberta-Saskatchewan border, and penetrated west to the shores of Lesser Slave Lake.

In the meantime, Crees also drove northward along the Athabasca River, pushing the Beavers back from Lake Claire to the Peace River. Because of an incident which took place during that time, the river received its current name.

> When this country was formerly invaded by the Knisteneaux [Cree], they found the Beaver Indians inhabiting the land about Portage la Loche; and the adjoining tribe were those whom they called slaves. They drove both these tribes before them; when the latter proceeded down the river from the Lake of the Hills [Lake Athabasca], in consequence of which that part of it obtained the name of the Slave River. The former [Beavers] proceeded up the river; and when the Knisteneaux made peace with them, this place was settled to be the boundary.

Alexander Mackenzie wrote this account at Peace Point, on the lower waters of Peace River, in 1792. By that time, the entire river was known as *Unijigah,* or Peace River.

In 1782, the Beaver Indians obtained

A small band of Beavers near the Peace River about 1899.

their first guns directly from European traders. Thus armed, they not only stemmed the Cree invasion, but they in turn pushed the ill-armed Sekanies out of the upper waters of the Peace and back into the mountains.

During the late 1700s and early 1800s, trading posts were built along the Peace River to serve the Beaver and Slavey tribes. The farthest upstream of these posts was Fort St. John, constructed in 1805, where it supplied both the Rocky Mountain Beavers and their enemies, the Senakies.

In 1823, this post was attacked by Beavers, the chief trader, Guy Hughes, and four of his men being killed and the fort being burned to the ground. Several stories exist as to the reason for the destruction. One is that the traders were going to relocate farther upstream, within the hunting grounds of the Senaki. Angered at thought of their enemies being provided with a steady supply of weapons and trade goods, the Beavers attacked. Another tale is that the Beaver were angry

about the liberties which the traders were taking with their women. Earlier, Mackenzie had observed that the Beaver "differ very much from the Chipewyans and Knisteneaux, in the abhorrence they profess of any carnal communication between their women and the white people." A third story is that Hughes poisoned an Indian boy and killed him.

Whatever the cause, the Hudson's Bay Co. decided to punish the Rocky Mountain Beavers by closing all the upriver posts for a period of three years. Any Indian who wished to trade had to make the long journey to Fort Vermilion. According to a Beaver Indian, his tribe "remained in the woods and did not visit a white man's house because they were afraid. From that time they . . . lived with their bows and arrows, not having gunpowder."

Yet the traders could not afford to keep the Beavers away from the posts for too long, for they were good providers. "No men in this land of hunters hunt better than the Beavers," commented a traveller in 1872. "It is not uncommon for a single Indian to render from his winter trapping 200 marten skins, and not less than 20,000 beavers are annually killed by the tribe on the waters of the Peace River."

As hunters, their favourite animal was the moose. Even though wood buffalo were available and were hunted when convenient, the tribe considered the moose to be their staple food. Caribou, bear and deer also were a source of meat. Smaller animals which were hunted for meat included rabbit and beaver; fish were caught but were not as important as they were to more northerly tribes. Other foods included berries of all kinds, a few roots, and the inner bark of certain trees.

Although one fur trader observed that the Beavers were "a peaceable and quiet People and perhaps the most honest of any on the face of the earth," they still had a reputation of being good fighters. Mackenzie noted that they "are more vicious and warlike than the Chepewyans" and their own folklore contains accounts of battles with the Cree and other enemies.

For example, a war party of Beavers, under the guidance of a medicine man, found an enemy camp towards the mountains west of Dunvegan. Crossing the river early in the morning, they were startled when a dog began to bark. "They all rushed forward thinking the camp would be alarmed by the dog," said Beaver informant John Bourassa. "They ran so fast one of the young men overtook the dog and killed it with a knife . . . They killed all [the enemy] but one man who ran and jumped in the river."

Little is known of the early religious life of the Beavers. Many of the ceremonies performed after their contact with Europeans had come recently from the Crees. As early as 1792, Mackenzie commented that "their religion is of a very contracted nature, and I never witnessed any ceremony of devotion which they had not borrowed from the Knisteneaux, their feasts and fasts being in imitation of that people."

Yet they did have supernatural helpers, particularly to assist men while hunting or going to war. Like other tribes, such helpers came to the men in dreams, the skins of animal helpers being worn to bring good luck and to ward off evil. They also used hunting charms, sometimes small effigy figures of the animals they sought. With starvation always a threat, great importance was attached to supernatural help in finding game.

Certain men took the role of healers or medicine men. They could find enemy camps, predict the success or failure of a Beaver war party, and cure the sick through incantations and rituals. Each band also had a prophet who was looked upon as the religious leader; such men might introduce new rituals as the result of dreams or visions.

A Beaver leader and his family in 1911.

Samson was a Beaver Indian dog team driver when photographed at Fort St. John about 1904.

A major ceremony which may have predated Cree influence was the "feeding the fire" ritual. Twice a year the prophet called the people together where a large dancing area had been cleared and a fire built in the centre. During the ritual, the holy man cast pieces of meat from game animals into the flames, praying that the tribe might always be fed from their flesh. He asked for rain and snow so that the animals would be easily tracked. After the prayers, an all-night dance was held in the open area, the men and women dancing in clockwise fashion around the blazing fire.

Information about the original costumes of the Beavers is scanty, for as early as 1809, fur trader Daniel Harmon noted that "the great part of them are now cloathed with European goods." The man's clothing was likely a long mooseskin coat or parka which extended to the knees. It had fitted sleeves and hood and was held in place by a belt. Other clothing consisted of a breechcloth, leggings and moccasins.

The women ornamented the clothing with beautiful designs in porcupine quillwork, later using beads and silk embroidery as well. They also made baskets of birchbark, incising them with attractive designs. The men made bows and arrows, sturdy canoes of birch or spruce bark, and toboggans.

The population of the Beavers showed a steady decline over the years, the tribe being affected by disease and starvation. In 1790, Mackenzie estimated there were 150 men in the tribe which, on a basis of seven per family, gave a tribal population of about 1,000. In 1889, Father Morice estimated the numbers to be 800; in 1906 there were 700, and in 1924, 600. By 1963 the population was further reduced to 560, but 20 years later it had grown to almost 1,000 persons.

After the Hudson's Bay Co. became well established along the Peace River, the Beavers drifted into the routine of hunting for food and trapping fur-bearing animals for the trade. Late each winter they visited the posts at Fort Vermilion, Dunvegan or Fort St. John, bartering their beaver, marten and other skins for ammunition, tobacco, utensils, cloth, and other supplies.

A description of a typical camp was provided in 1872 by William F. Butler.

> On the morning of the third day after leaving [Fort] Vermilion we fell in with a band of Beavers. Five wigwams stood pitched upon a pretty rising knoll, backed by pine woods, which skirted the banks of the stream, upon the channel of which the lodges of the animal beaver rose cone-like above the snow. When we reached the camp, 'At-tal-loo', the chief, came forth. A stranger was a rare sight and 'At-tal-loo' was bound to make a speech; three of his warriors, half a dozen children, and a few women filled up the background. Leaning upon a long single-barrelled gun 'At-tal-loo' began . . .
>
> This winter had been a severe one; death had struck heavily into the tribe; in these

three wigwams six women had died . . . Tea was the pressing want. Without tea the meat of the moose was insipid . . .

I endeavoured to find out the cause of this mortality among the poor hunters, and it was not far to seek. Constitutions enfeebled by close intermarriage, and by the hardships attending upon wild life in these northern regions, were fast wearing out. At the present rate of mortality the tribe of the Beavers will soon be extinct, and with them will have disappeared the best and the simplest of the nomad tribes of the north.

In 1899, after the invasion of prospectors going north to the Klondike had caused considerable antagonism among the Beaver and other tribes, the Canadian government negotiated a treaty with Indians of northern Alberta and northeastern British Columbia. A treaty commission party set out from Edmonton in June and after meeting with Crees at Lesser Slave Lake, it proceeded on to meet the Beavers at Fort St. John. However, the date conflicted with the annual hunt so the independent Beavers decided not to wait for them.

Disappointed, for the Beavers in that area were more primitive than their more easterly cousins and had experienced considerable trouble with prospectors, the commissioners went back to Dunvegan, where the 34 Beaver Indians under the leadership of Natooses signed the treaty. In the meantime, another segment of the official party went to Peace River Landing where Duncan Tastawits signed on behalf of the 47 Beavers and Crees there. Proceeding north for Fort Vermilion, further approval of the treaty was obtained from Beaver chiefs Ambrose Tete Noire and Pierrot Fournier on behalf of their 148 followers.

"The Indians with whom we treated differ in many respects from the Indians of the organized territories," commented the official party. "They indulge in neither paint not feathers, and never clothe themselves in blankets. Their dress is of the ordinary style and many of them were well clothed. In the summer they live in teepees, but many of them have log

Furs traded from the Beaver Indians are piled in packs in front of this trading post about 1904. Operated by Bredin & Cornwall, it was located at Fort St. John.

houses in which they live in winter . . . All the Indians we met were with rare exceptions professing Christians, and showed evidences of the work which missionaries have carried on among them for many years."

When the official party returned to Edmonton, the Beavers at Fort St. John still were unsigned. Not until the following spring was a meeting arranged between Commissioner J. A. Macrae and the Rocky Mountain band. A total of 46 Beavers were admitted into treaty, the document being signed by Muckithay, Aginaa, Dislisici, Tachea, Appan, Attachie, Allalie, and Yatsoose. With that adhesion, on May 30, 1900, the last of the Beaver tribe had accepted Treaty No. Eight.

Although they had surrendered their lands in exchange for treaty money, reserves and other benefits, the way of life of the Beavers did not change immediately. Not until later did the bands take reserves at Fort St. John and Hudson Hope in British Columbia, and at Boyer River, Horse Lake and Clear Hills in Alberta.

For example, in 1913, the Beavers at Fort Vermilion selected their reserve at Boyer River, with a smaller one being located nearby at Child's Lake. Typical comments of the Indian agent in that year are as follows:

The Peace River Crossing band of Beavers and Crees had a reserve at Old Wives Lake. They lived by farming, hunting and freighting, and were considered "temperate and fairly moral." The Beavers at Fort St. John had no reserve, many were suffering from tuberculosis, and they were very poor. They still lived in tepees, had few horses and "they do not progress." Those at Dunvegan had a reserve but spent most of their time hunting. A few had log houses and gardens, but most of them lived in tepees and were a "peaceable" people.

In later years, as health and educational services improved, the Beavers began to grow in numbers and to find additional employment in the area. The introduction of registered trap lines and the decline of game animals also changed the way of life of these once nomadic people.

This group of Beaver Indians, seen at Little Red River in 1919, lived by hunting and fishing.

SLAVEY INDIANS

The Slavey Indians are the most northerly tribe in Alberta, their hunting grounds extending well into the Northwest Territories. Known as *Acha'otinne*, or "woodland people," they are of Athapascan linguistic stock and are closely related to the Beavers. They received the name "Slave" or "Slavey" *(Awokanak)* as a derisive expression from the enemy Cree, but today, they refer to themselves as *Dene Chaa* or *Dene Thaa*.

According to explorer Alexander Mackenzie, the Slaveys originally inhabited the area west of Lake Athabasca but retreated northward in the 1700s when the Crees, armed with guns from the traders, moved westward and northward. By the end of the century, most of the tribe was congregated west of Great Slave Lake and along the Mackenzie River. However, they still continued to penetrate into the Caribou Mountains and Hay River of northern Alberta, an area they considered to be part of their hereditary hunting grounds.

They were divided into six bands, which were identified by their geographical locations, the Horn Mountain, Hay River, Peace River, Forks, Rapids, and Mackenzie River bands. None had formal chiefs but wandered through their areas in small family groups. Only in time of war was one man given responsibility of leadership for his band, but as soon as peace was restored, he reverted to his former position as a hunter.

Although in dress and habits they were similar to the Beavers and Chipewyans, the Slaveys nevertheless had a number of distinctive traits. One of these was to avoid the barrenlands to the north-east, even during periods when caribou was plentiful in that area. Their preference for the wooded areas gave rise to their name, woodland people.

Life was difficult for the tribe and starvation was not uncommon. Fish was one of their principal foods, particularly during the winter months. A hole was

A Slavey Indian woman displays some of her beadwork about 1900.

made in the ice of a lake and a spruce root net stretched through the water to another hole where the trapped fish were brought to the surface. Other fish were caught with hooks and lines or with weirs made of stones or brush.

Because fish was so important to their diet, the Slaveys either ate it fresh or dried it in the sun for future use. The most popular methods of cooking were roasting over an open fire or boiling in watertight baskets suspended high above the flames.

A Slavey woman fishes through the ice on Hay River.

Second only to fish were moose and caribou. Often the annual cycles of a band depended upon the location of the big game animals, which were most easily killed in the spring, when they were trapped in deep snow. The Slaveys were considered excellent moose hunters, being familiar with their habits and showing great skill in tracking them.

Other foods eaten by the tribe included rabbits, lynx, squirrels, muskrat, beaver, bear, all kinds of waterfowl and upland game, birds' eggs, and such berries as raspberry, cranberry and crowberry.

The clothing worn by the Slaveys was similar to that of the Chipewyan and Beaver, but was more lavish in appearance. Not only did they use more fringes,

but clothing was much more highly decorated with moose hair embroidery and dyed porcupine quills. Similarly, when European trade goods were introduced, the women made great use of beads, tassels and other forms of ornamentation.

In 1810, trader George Keith described a man's costume as follows:

> Their summer dress consists of a leather shirt with long fringes, before and behind, neatly garnished with coloured moose hair and porcupine quills. Around the waist, they have a belt neatly wrought with porcupine quills; they wear long necklaces with fringes; their leggings and shoes go with the rest.

And of the women he stated:

> The tender sex, of course, strives to excel in this particular and are sometimes covered

with fringes, almost from head to foot. A young or middle aged widow wears long leggings or breaches as a protection. The winter dresses are made of fur.

Traders considered the Slaveys to be a peaceful and timid people, yet there were instances of them fighting with their neighbours, the Dogribs, and with the more aggressive Crees who were considered to be enemies. The Slaveys also drove the Nahanni Indians west into the mountains and later destroyed a trading post at Fort Nelson.

Religious ceremonies in the tribe were of an individual nature, with hunters seeking guardian spirits which would enable them to kill moose and other game. Often such a spirit was in the form of an animal which revealed itself to the hunter in a dream; from that time on, the man would not eat the flesh of that creature but usually carried its skin as a sacred object. He would also perform certain secret rituals which had been taught to him by his guardian helper.

Surrounded by hardship and possible starvation, the Slaveys placed great faith in these helpers to dispel the evil spirits. Similarly there were conjurers in the tribe who could locate game, cast spells on enemies, cure the sick, and foretell the future. The ability of these men was well known among neighbouring tribes, and in spite of the fact that the Slaveys were a quiet and inoffensive people, they often were feared because of these supernatural powers.

Yet life was not all hardship and superstition. The Slaveys enjoyed dancing, in fact they preferred it to gambling as a pastime. Boys liked to wrestle and often this method was used to settle disputes, particularly in the choice of a bride.

"They live in lodges," said George Keith, describing Slavey social life, "generally two families to a lodge, one on each side of the fire. The women seldom prepare the lodge in winter, or go for wood unless the husband is absent, and the men perform all the hard labours, so indulgent they are to the women. All partake of the same mess [and] although sometimes compelled to eat rank and putrid provisions, they are very careful in cutting up an animal, to cut away all obnoxious matter or glands, and, in summer, they often renew their bark dishes."

The Slaveys were fond of story telling, the tales often being lessons in life for the children. Others were legends relating to the origin of the earth and the creatures upon it. Here is an example, recorded in 1808:

One day the sun disappeared and heavy snow threatened to kill everyone on earth. At last, a party of Slaveys set out to discover what had happened. During their travels they met a squirrel who told them that the sun had been stolen by a she bear who lived in a beautiful land far away. Joining the Indians, the squirrel led them to the bear's lodge where they saw two cubs playing outside, near a long babiche line which led into the sky. Tied to the cord were five mysterious bags.

A young Slavey couple at Hay River proudly show their first baby, about 1900.

79

Observing that the mother bear was across the lake hunting, the travellers captured the cubs and forced them to reveal what was inside the five bags. The lower one contained snow, the next rain, and the next two, thunder and the stars. The cubs would not tell the contents of the last bag, but after being threatened with death, they admitted that it held the sun.

The squirrel called upon a pike, methy-fish and mouse to help them. The fish were instructed to rescue the sun, while the mouse was to cross the lake and chew the bear's paddle half through. The pike brought the bag to earth just as the mouse returned, and the little animal quickly chewed a hole in it. In the meantime, the bear noticed the strangers in her camp, but as she set out in her canoe to cross the lake, her paddle broke. Then, as she roared in anger, the sun flashed out of the bag and filled the sky.

The bear could not bring the sun back, but she still had the power to command it, so she instructed it to shine down brightly upon the snow-covered land. The sudden heat caused the snow to melt, and soon the earth was covered by great flood waters. Even the adventurous travellers were caught and only a man and his wife were able to reach a high mountain peak. There they found animals and birds gathered against the great flood.

After several days, the waters were still so high that the survivors began to starve, so the man sent a duck to dive into the water to find the earth. When it was unsuccessful, he sent a loon, which likewise could not reach the bottom. At last a buzzard was sent below and returned unconscious with its beak full of earth. In the days that followed, the buzzard continued to dive, each time showing that the earth was getting closer and closer, until at last there was dry land, and everyone was free.

The first contact between Slavey Indians and European traders probably took place shortly after 1778, when a trading post was opened on Lake Athabasca. Prior to that time, other tribes such as the Chipewyans had been trading on the shores of Hudson Bay and in turn had sold European objects to the Slaveys for great profits. The traders were aware that

Two Slaveys paddle the Slave River near Fitzgerald in 1926.

A Slavey camp of tepees and cabins was located close to the banks of Hay River in 1898.

there were tribes farther west of the Chipewyans, for in the 1760s, Andrew Graham observed "There are many natives that inhabit a large tract of country to the NW of the Copper-mine River, known by the name of Copper Indians, and Strongbowed Indians, and there are beyond them other natives who use stone axes, arrow-heads, etc."

In order to contact these tribes, posts were built on Lake Athabasca and north into the Mackenzie River system. Soon the Slaveys were using metal tools, guns, copper kettles, twine nets, beads and other goods. However, in order to obtain these objects, they changed their whole pattern of life; instead of following an annual cycle in search of fish and meat, they turned to trapping and the snaring of fur bearing animals as their livelihood.

Yet the land was sufficiently remote from the southerly fur trading routes that the Slaveys remained relatively undisturbed for the next one hundred years. Their life centred around their camps and the trading posts until the first missionaries arrived. The earliest to visit them was Bishop W. C. Bompas, who began work for the Anglicans in the Mackenzie district in 1865. He was followed a short time later by Oblate missionaries, and soon most of the trading posts had small mission stations nearby.

In 1899, the Canadian government arranged to negotiate Treaty No. Eight with the Athapascan and northern Cree tribes. Although the treaty party travelled as far north as Fort Vermilion, the Slavey bands which hunted on the upper waters of Hay River decided not to attend. In the following year, however, they appeared at the fort and affixed their adhesion to the treaty. Those signing on behalf of the 178 members of the band were Alexis Tatatechay, Francois Tchatee, Giroux Nahdayyah, Koka, and Kachweesala.

A few days later, the treaty party continued on to Fort Resolution, in the Northwest Territories, where two Slavey chiefs, Sunrise and Lamelise, signed on behalf of 104 Indians who hunted near the mouth of Hay River.

The other bands in the tribe, which normally hunted farther north towards Great Bear Lake, were not included in Treaty No. Eight, and in 1902 the Indian Inspector commented that "The Indians on the north side of Great Slave Lake are anxious to come into treaty, as are those of Providence on the Mackenzie River. They claim that the Slaveys and Yellowknives, who were taken into treaty in

1900, have hunting grounds outside of treaty and are akin to them." However, not until 1921 was a separate agreement, Treaty No. Eleven, negotiated with the Slaveys farther north. This included 258 people at Fort Providence, 347 at Fort Simpson, 78 at Wrigley, and 208 at Fort Norman. In the following year, another 150 Slaveys at Fort Liard signed an adhesion to the treaty.

By the time all negotiations had been completed, a total of 1,323 Slaveys had been admitted into treaty. This compares closely to the estimated population of 1,250 for the tribe in the pre-European period, indicating that the peaceful Slaveys had maintained a relatively stable population as long as they remained hunters and fishermen.

Within a few years, however, the inroads of tuberculosis and other diseases caused a rapid reduction in the population of the tribe. In 1928, for example, a visitor to Fort Norman commented that

Two Slavey girls, about 1919.

"At that place during the following fortnight an epidemic of influenza killed a large part of the Indian population," and in the following year a Hudson's Bay trader at Sikkani Post predicted that the tribe would soon be extinct. "Round his own district," said the *Edmonton Journal* in an interview with William Gairdner, "where a few years ago there were some 50 trappers of the Slavey Indian tribe, today there are about eight." Soon the Slaveys had decreased to an estimated population of 800 persons and remained at a low ebb until improved health services were provided after World War Two. By 1983, the population had increased to 4,081 persons.

At the same time, the postwar years were difficult ones. The scarcity of fur bearing animals, limitation of fishing, and the concentration of families near government schools meant a breakdown in the old way of life.

Yet the improved educational service gave many young Slaveys an opportunity to learn new skills, some moving as far away as Edmonton to seek work. Others have been engaged in a number of northern enterprises, ranging from employment in towns, to working in oil projects, commercial fishing and transportation.

In 1807, fur trader W. F. Wentzel made the following observation about the Slaveys' character: "Their dispositions are sociable, mild and harmless; they never make war with their neighbours and never quarrel with the Whites; they are submissive and very obedient, perhaps through ignorance . . . yet generally good natured, courteous to strangers, peaceable among themselves and easily contented."

In some respects, these characteristics of mildness and sociability enabled the Slaveys to easily accept the changes which have taken place in their lives. At the same time, the Twentieth Century has not treated them kindly.

OJIBWA INDIANS

The Ojibwa Indians were known by several names — the Chippewa, Saulteaux, Soto, or Bungee. They are of Algonkian linquistic stock and historically inhabited the area near the Great Lakes, particularly north of Lake Superior. They were fairly closely related to the Cree and generally were on good terms with them.

Because of the location of their hunting grounds, the Ojibwa encountered fur traders at an early date and discovered the profits to be made by devoting their attention to trapping. Aggressively, and with the encouragement of the North West Company, they began to move out from their traditional areas, seeking furs in new lands. During this same period the Sioux, their moral enemies, migrated south-westward onto the plains, leaving more territory open for expansion. The result was that whole bands were slowly moving west while, at the same time, traders were hiring individual Ojibwas to go farther West to trap for them.

Trader Peter Fidler, when discussing the Ojibwas in the West commented:

> These Indians are not originally natives of these Parts, but were first introduced by the North West Company about the year 1797 —before this there were a very few Straglers —they being then Industerous [sic] they was induced by the Reports of the Canadians that Beaver abounded here & was invited to leave their original Lands about the Rain[y] Lake & the Western borders of Lake Superior — now they finding this Country so much more plentiful in Provisions than their own & the Beaver being plentiful — they have become quite habituated to these parts & I believe will never return to their own Lands again.

This was the time when the North West Co. and Hudson's Bay Co. were experiencing keen competition from small trading firms organized in Montreal. In order to destroy them, they decided to import Ojibwa and Iroquois Indians to trap the beaver areas and, at the same time, to open a whole string of tiny trading posts which the small firms could never match.

In 1794 a number of Ojibwas were trapping in the Edmonton area and two years later several families moved to the upper waters of the North Saskatchewan to trap. At the same time, there was an active band of both Ojibwa and Ottawa Indians in the Lac La Biche district. They were an outgoing, proud group who intimidated the local Indians with their shamanism and demanded that the fur traders stock special goods for them. At Edmonton in 1798 the factor reported that the "Bungee Indians traded forty-five beaver, twenty of which was for silver work; they wanted wampum very much which I was sorry to inform them there was none."

Peter Fidler, who traded throughout the West, noted their fascination for silver:

> . . . some of the young Bungee Men are very flashy & decorated with a variety of Silver ornaments in the Summer Months, such as necklaces made of whampum about 2 Inches broad, arm and wrist bands with gorgets, Broaches, &c., Scarlet Leggins garnished with Ribbands and Beads and a number of small Brooches, which is very tastefully arranged.

When the competition from the little companies ended between 1804 and 1807, the need for Ojibwa and Iroquois trappers ended. Besides, so aggressively had they gone through the country that beaver were becoming scarce. Although most of the Ojibwas returned to the East, a few decided to remain. In 1821, for example, there were estimated to be some

This group of Ojibwa Indians was sketched near Red River in Manitoba in 1870.

thirty Ojibwa hunters and trappers in the Peace River area and over the next few decades, small parties drifted into the region as people from Manitoba began to migrate west.

The Rev. Robert Rundle, a Methodist missionary, noted in 1841 that a group of these Indians had adapted to prairie life and that most of the other Indians were afraid of them because of their spiritual powers. He observed at Fort Edmonton that

> Several of the Souteaux Indians left in the morning to hunt buffalo because I had preached on the previous evening against their idolatries. They pretended to have intercourse with familiar spirits & thereby held the other Indians in terror with their pretended divinations & enchantments.

Six years later, when artist Paul Kane went through the area, he encountered small bands of mixed Ojibwa-Cree trading at Fort Pitt. One of these was led by an Ojibwa named Black Powder whose son,

Big Bear, became a famous figure in Canadian history. Black Powder and his son both had become adapted to the plains and hunted in eastern Alberta in the Wainwright, Sounding Lake, and Empress areas. In later years these people planned to take a reserve at Frog Lake but because of their role in the Riel Rebellion of 1885, Big Bear was imprisoned and his band dispersed.

In spite of the fact that there were families of Ojibwas scattered throughout the woodland areas of Alberta, only one group ever established a reserve, and this didn't happen until 1950.

In the early 1880s, when the buffalo were destroyed, many Indians in Saskatchewan were forced to go far out onto the prairies in search of food. Two such bands were under the leadership of *Pewaysis*, or Thunder, and *Tatwasin*, or Breaking Through the Ice, who took their followers to the plains near the Cypress Hills. Most of them had never accepted treaty.

84

While in the south, the Ojibwas camped near Maple Creek and Fort Walsh and travelled far into Montana in search of buffalo. Finally, Fort Walsh was closed and the Indians were left to starve.

In desperation, *Tatwasin* and Thunder took their followers to Buffalo Lake, south-east of Edmonton, where they met a band of non-treaty Crees. Nearby was the Peace Hills Indian Agency, which looked after the Indians at Hobbema, but because the visitors did not belong, they were seldom fed. During the winter of 1884-85, the Indian agent enquired whether these Indians should be encouraged to take a reserve.

> They say they are going to work there. If it is your intention to allow them to stay there, Implements, Provisions, etc. will have to be furnished very early this spring . . . [The Crees] have done very little this winter to help themselves. The Salteaux are very little better though since I refused them supplies they have kept away.

However, the Riel Rebellion occurred before any action could be taken; Thunder and *Tatwasin* took no part in the uprising but built cabins and prepared to settle down. At first, the government thought the reserve was a good idea "as then those who are scattered along the Railway at Medicine Hat and other points would join Pe-ua-sis [Thunder]." However, nothing was done and finally in 1887 *Tatwasin's* group decided to leave Buffalo Lake because of a lack of food. That autumn, a man at Red Deer observed that "forty lodges of Saulteau Indians passed through for the Rocky Mountain Fort. They are migrating from Buffalo lakes." Because of starvation and government inaction, the Ojibwas had found a new home on the upper waters of the North Saskatchewan River.

In the 1880s there was very little settlement beyond the railway lines, so the Ojibwas were left alone. No attempt was made to force them onto reserves nor were they disturbed from their traditional hunting life. They travelled over a vast area, hunting deer and antelope on the prairie, fishing in the north, and wintering in the foothills.

In 1901, a white settler noted the existence of these wandering Indians.

> . . . in this district exists a band of Saulteaux Indians who simply live on the slaughter of . . . game. This band I understand came from Manitoba some years ago and have made their wandering homes between the Red Deer river and north as far as the Beaver hills but principally around the Battle river. There are about twenty families . . . who will not take treaty. If I am not mistaken this is the same band that has for years past slaughtered deer, elk and moose in the Beaver Hills during fly time in summer.

Of course, this man was interested in hunting only for sport, so he resented these nomadic people. He complained

Ojibwa woman with her child in a cradleboard, 1880s.

that they had killed an elk "very old and thin but with an enormous head. The latter through superstition was left on the prairie to rot. What a trophy this is for a white man."

As the area along the Battle River and Beaver Hills became cultivated, the Ojibwas remained more and more in the wooded foothills. There they were joined by the band of Crees which had come from the Cypress Hills and was now under the leadership of Sun Child. Already resident in the area were the Stoneys, who had a reserve at Morley. These three groups lived harmoniously in the foothills, intermarrying, and eking out a precarious existence.

For several years, the Indians relied on hunting, trapping, and the sale of handicrafts and berries for subsistence. Upon the death of *Tatwasin,* the leadership was taken by his brother, Jim O'Chiese, who was strongly opposed to settling on a reserve and cautioned his followers to maintain their independence. When the chief's death occurred in 1931, the control of Alberta's natural resources had been transferred from the federal to the provincial government and there was a fear that all the good Crown land would be taken up. Accordingly, in spite of the fact that the Indians had not asked for them, the government set up two reserves northwest of Rocky Mountain House for the future use of the O'Chiese Ojibwas and the Sun Child Crees. At first, the Indians seriously considered accepting the reserves but they were afraid their children would be taken away from them and sent to boarding schools, and that the people would be no longer free to roam.

In 1944 the Sun Child Crees finally went to their reserve, but the Ojibwas continued to hold out. Many drifted north to the Edson area where they found work in sawmills and with local ranchers.

When the Sun Child Crees accepted treaty in the 1940s, a number of Ojibwas attended the ceremonies. Joe Strawberry, one of their leaders, is standing at right.

An Ojibwa Indian, Kishwan Strawberry, receives his treaty money at Rocky Mountain House in 1950.

Others stayed at their favourite campsites along the Baptiste River where they had lived for many years. In 1946 and 1947, the government tried to persuade the current chief, John O'Chiese, to sign the treaty, but he steadfastly refused. Finally, a group of fifteen families under Andrew Strawberry broke away in 1950 and accepted the terms of the agreement. When they moved to their reserve, they were given horses, cattle, farm equipment, and help in building houses.

John O'Chiese never did agree to settle on the reserve and at the time of his death in 1951 he was with his non-treaty followers near Hinton, Alberta. His son, Peter, carried on the tradition for many years and when he was interviewed in 1959, he explained why he remained free and independent.

> All our lives we have been used to eating wild game animals, game birds and fish. The flesh of domesticated animals and the fish which is sold in butcher shops does not satisfy our craving, as does that which God has supplied for our use. Surely we non-Treaty Chippewa Indians who have never bartered our rights to this country are as much entitled to take wild big game as the predatory animals. We are law-abiding people; we were here for many generations before white people came to this country. We have never relinquished our rights in those districts in which we lived, hunted and trapped.
>
> My father and grandfather were not in favor of signing treaty and seeing their people in a reservation or, as my grandfather referred to it, 'As being corralled like cattle.' So when you talk to me about signing Treaty and bringing the remnants of our people into a reservation, I can only reply by saying that we are not ready to sacrifice our lives . . .

Some of the Ojibwas never did accept treaty and continue to work and hunt in the area east of Jasper National Park. Those who moved onto their reserve gradually settled in to their new life. By 1985 the reserve had a population of 377 persons, predominantly Ojibwa, but with a representation of Cree as well. Today, the administration of the reserve is in the hands of band members and farming has replaced hunting and trapping as its main occupation.

IROQUOIS INDIANS

The Iroquois are not an Indian tribe which was native to western Canada; rather, they were an eastern Woodlands people who were brought in by the fur trading companies. During the latter part of the 18th century, the North West Company engaged a number of "Nepissings, the Algonquins and Iroquois Indians" from the Montreal area to act as boatmen and to trap for furs in the West.

These Indians had begun to use steel traps in the 1790s and had been so successful in taking foxes and other animals that the Nor-Westers believed they could do equally well with the more valuable beaver pelts in the West. At that time, western Indians used deadfalls or dug beavers out of their lodges.

The first group of hunters proved to be very successful. As David Thompson commented in 1800, these Indians "now spread themselves over these countries, and as they destroyed the Beaver, moved forwards to the northward and westward. For several years all these Indians were rich . . ." This initial group was followed by others. In the summer of 1801, the North West Co. brought in more Iroquois on three-year contracts "to complete the destruction of the beaver which had already been started several years back . . ." However, the rapid destruction of the beaver by these foreign Indians caused considerable anger among the local tribes.

Shortly after their arrival, a party of 14 Iroquois on their way to Chesterfield House were attacked and killed by Gros Ventre Indians. Farther north, the Carrier Indians killed an Iroquois in 1818, causing Daniel Harmon to comment:

> For several years past, Iroquois from Canada, have been in the habit of coming into different parts of the North West country, to hunt the beaver, &c. The Natives of the country consider them as intruders. . . . the Indians here, have often threatened to kill them, if they persisted in destroying the animals on their lands.

This Iroquois Indian came west as a trapper and then set out on his own when his contract expired. He was painted by Alfred Jacob Miller in 1837.

The first Iroquois were treated by the traders as valuable employees, partly because they were believed to be more "civilized" than local Indians and also because of their willingness to work for the trading companies. Even when their contracts expired, many of the Iroquois decided to remain in the West, hunting as "freemen" in the foothills and the north.

Some of the Iroquois preferred to remain in the employ of the traders, performing the tasks of boatmen and hunters. For example, in 1804, records showed several Iroquois working for the North West Company, such as Paul Cheney-echoe, Ignace Nowaniouter, and Jacques Quiter Tisato on the Athabasca River; and Louis Calihue, Ignace Saliohony, and P. Cawandawa at Fort Edmonton.

These early Iroquois brought many of their tribal practises with them. When a group of them were setting out to attack an enemy, they performed a war dance and painted themselves for battle, just as the western Indians did. David Thompson also observed that they had their own pipe dance and gambling games.

Yet of the several hundred Iroquois men who came west, there were few if any women. Thompson claimed there had been some with the first group, all wives of hunters, but others say the men came alone. As a result, they tended to marry women from local tribes, one of the most popular being the Cree. Other individuals crossed the mountains where they established firm relations with the Sikani, Shuswap, and other tribes. One of these Iroquois, Pierre Bostonnais, left an indelible mark on the country when his nickname, Tete Jaune or Yellowhead, was chosen as a name for a mountain pass. However, he did not live to glorify in his fame, as he and his brother were killed by local Indians in 1827.

More lasting fame came to the men who became the founders of the Iroquois families in Alberta. Born at Caughnaw-

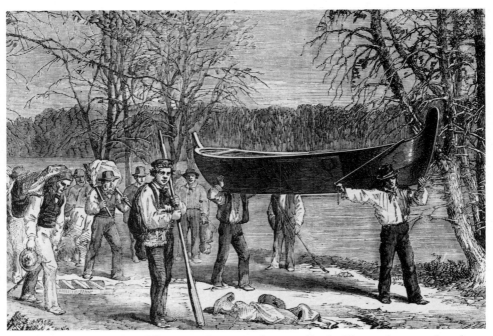

Charlot Skanasah, with paddle, was an Iroquois who stayed in the West and was employed as a guide when this sketch was made in 1858.

This child, Danny Wanyande, was a descendent of the original Iroquois from Montreal. He is seen here at Grande Cache in 1919.

they ranged along the foothills as far north as the Peace River but spent much of their time in the Jasper and Grande Cache areas. Father Jean De Smet met them at Jasper in 1845, and ten years later, Father Lacombe made a special trip to see them when they asked for a priest.

> I passed fifteen days with them, teaching day and night, and baptising, marrying, and giving the sacraments to the happy people of the mountain. I met some of the old Iroquois, the founders of the colony. The last who survived was named Joachim. He had yet with him, as precious relics, his prayer-book in Iroquois, and other articles of piety he brought with him from Montreal.

Later, many of the Iroquois moved near the Catholic mission at Lac Ste. Anne, and from there they hunted and trapped throughout the region. Others remained at Grande Cache. By this time, Father Lacombe noted that the Iroquois language was almost extinct among them, and that they spoke only Cree and French. Many of the group were Cree half-breeds.

Louis Callihoo was an acknowledged leader of the band and upon his death his son, Michel, became chief. He worked off and on for the Hudson's Bay Co., travelling as far east as Winnipeg with their boats. Usually, however, he preferred to hunt and trap in the Lac Ste. Anne region.

When the Indians of the North Saskatchewan signed Treaty No. Six at Fort Pitt and Fort Carlton in 1876, Callihoo and his band did not bother to attend the ceremonies. However, two years later, Michel signed an adhesion to the treaty and at the following annuity payments his band consisted of 231 persons. Other than Callihoo, most of the band had such Metis names as Gladieu, L'Hirondelle, and Valade. A year later, 1880, they moved to Michel's Reserve, sixteen miles northwest of Edmonton near Riviere Qui Barre.

A number of these native settlers had already learned the techniques of farming

aga, on the outskirts of Montreal, these men included Louis Karhiio (or Callihoo), Ignace Karakwante, and their cousin, Ignace Wanyande. Of the forty men in their original party, eighteen were killed by Blackfoot Indians and most of the remainder returned east when their contracts expired. But the three men decided to remain and trap on their own in the foothills. According to Father Lacombe, after working at Fort Edmonton "they bought a large outfit of ammunition, traps, knives, axes, blankets, etc., and left Edmonton to go and hunt for themselves in the direction of the Rocky Mountains, at the head of the Athabasca River."

Later, they were joined by Joachim Tonatanhan who came West in 1818. These men married local women, mostly from the Cree tribe and joined forces with local half-breeds. Hunting and trapping, from the missionaries, so they wasted no time in establishing small farms. When an Indian Department inspector visited the reserve in 1884, he was enthusiastic.

> The crops upon this reserve are excellent, and one cannot realize that he is driving through an Indian reserve. The large fields, strong, straight fences, and good log houses, in the midst of a surrounding country of mixed wood and prairie, almost lead one to fancy that he is passing through some of the newly settled districts of Ontario.

This was only one of many indications that these people were different from Indians on other nearby reserves. When a governor-general visited the area in the early 1890s and was introduced to Michel Callihoo and his brother, he commented:

John Callihoo, seen here in 1952, was long-time chief of Michel's Reserve and founder of the Indian Association of Alberta.

"These men are not of the Cree tribe."

"No," replied the Indian agent, "they are not Cree, they are Iroquois."

By the turn of the century, the Indian agent believed that their Iroquois heritage had virtually disappeared. "Thirteen families, numbering sixty-six individuals," he said, "can trace descent from one or other of these brothers and, as no women came with the original immigrants, it is obvious that the Iroquois blood in this generation is attenuated to the vanishing point. They have lost their language, and if they retain any tribal characteristics they have become so feeble that the ordinary observer of Indian manners is unable to discern them."

The Iroquois also were different in their attitude to the Indian Department. Whereas many Indians believed they had to obey the government or they would starve to death, the Callihoo people were self-sufficient and self assured enough to constantly fight with Indian agents. One of their leaders, John Callihoo, was given the nickname "The Lawyer" because of his ability to argue with the bureaucrats. He later became the driving force in organizing a political action group, the Indian Association of Alberta.

In fact, the Iroquois were so independent that they believed the only way they could be free of government interference was to give up their legal status. They tried in 1931 and again in 1949 to remove their reserve from government control. Finally, in 1958, they renounced their status, took possession of their reserve, and legally ceased to be Indians. They were the only Indians in Alberta ever to take such a step. As a result, Michel's Reserve no longer exists and those descendents of the small group of Iroquois trappers are now part of the larger Canadian community. Other descendants who remained at Grande Cache or joined bands farther north have followed the traditional life of a woodland people.

GROS VENTRE INDIANS

The Gros Ventre Indians were variously known as the Gros Ventres du Prairie, Atsina, Fall, and Waterfall Indians. They once had been part of the Arapaho tribe but had split off from them and moved to the Canadian prairies.

The earliest fur traders found them in west-central Saskatchewan where they were closely allied to the Blackfoot tribes. In 1793, Cree Indians who were friendly to the traders attacked and destroyed a band of sixteen Gros Ventre lodges, so in retaliation, the Indians plundered the Hudson's Bay Co. trading post Manchester House and a year later destroyed South Branch House.

Fearing retaliation, the Gros Ventres began to move south-west from their old hunting grounds and started to trade at Edmonton House. Late in 1796, the first camp of more than 400 Gros Ventre Indians arrived at Edmonton and were relieved when the traders made peace and took about a thousand of their beaver skins in trade.

However, relations between the traders and Indians remained uneasy. In 1801, the Gros Ventres were devastated when Cree and Stoney Indians attacked their camps, killing 76 men, women, and child-

Three Gros Ventre warriors prepare for a mock battle at their Fort Belknap Reservation in Montana.

A Gros Ventre woman prepares a feast for a grass dance.

ren. This was followed by a smallpox epidemic which wiped out another 100 people, and a bitterly cold winter which caused further suffering and hardship. Blaming the Europeans for many of their problems, the Gros Ventres killed 14 fur trade employees on their way to Chesterfield House, near the present Empress, Alberta, in the spring of 1802 and the factor at the fort was afraid of a full scale war.

> . . . three or four Fall Indians rapped at their gates about midnight and wanted admittance, which was granted. When the gates were open upwards of seventy Fall Indian men all well-armed rushed into the yard and choked up the men's house nearly. All the Canadians was obliged to arm and was very near firing upon the Fall Indians in the house; when they saw the several of them must inevitably fall, they all thought proper to go away without doing any kind of violence.

Later in the year, the traders learned that the Gros Ventres had gone south to the Missouri River to meet the Crow and Arapaho Indians to form an alliance "and that they will then come to fall upon us and proceed down the country to find the Crees and Stone Indians and kill what they can of them." As a result, Chesterfield House was abandoned.

The Gros Ventres resumed trading at Edmonton but as American traders followed the Lewis and Clark expedition to the Upper Missouri area, the tribe gradually moved southwards. In 1815, a trader at Edmonton indicated that their hunting grounds were bounded on the north by the Bow and South Saskatchewan rivers, west to the present Lethbridge, east to the Saskatchewan border and southward into Montana. Within a few years, however, they were hunting and trading exclusively in the United States and had no further involvement north of the border. The tribe now lives on the Fort Belknap Reservation in eastern Montana.

SHOSHONI, KOOTENAY AND CROW INDIANS

Immediately prior to the first Europeans arriving in the West, there is evidence that southern Alberta was occupied by the Shoshoni, Kootenay, and Crow Indians. Traditions of the Blackfoot are consistent in saying that at one time these tribes occupied all of Alberta south of the Bow River.

One elderly Blood Indian stated:

> The Blackfeet at one time were all one people. From the North Saskatchewan to the Bow River was their hunting grounds, while the Snakes lived south of the Bow. The Kootenays had the area around the Porcupine Hills while the Crow Indians had the land which makes up the present Blood Reserve.

The Shoshoni are a tribe of Uto-Aztecan linguistic stock who historically occupied the mountain area in the Idaho-Wyoming region. They were known to the Blackfoot and many other tribes as the Snake Indians; in Plains Indian sign language, the figure of a snake represented this tribe.

Explorer David Thompson, who spent the winter of 1787-88 with the Peigans on the Bow River, said that the Blackfoot hunting grounds had been in possession of the two tribes, with the Kootenays to the north and the Snakes south of them. About 1730, the Blackfoot acquired their first guns and began to drive the Snakes away. Thompson was told stories about "the battles they had fought to gain the country of the Bow River." However, the Shoshonis retaliated when they obtained their first horses from tribes farther south. In the end, however, either warfare or disease caused the Shoshonis to withdraw to the south-west.

According to one Indian, the Blackfoot and Shoshini had been friendly but became enemies when a Shoshoni boy was injured in a game.

The opposing forces of Snakes and Blackfeet confronted each other on opposite sides

A Shoshoni woman was sketched at Fort Union by Karl Bodmer in 1833.

of the Bow River near present Gleichen, Alberta. A Snake Indian challenged a member of the Blackfoot party to meet him in single combat. Scabby Robe [a Blackfoot] answered his challenge and the two met in the middle of the river. The Snake threw his [lance] at Scabby Robe. It missed, and Scabby Robe picked it up and killed the Snake with his own weapon . . . From that time on there was continuous warfare between the Snakes and Blackfeet.

By the time fur traders arrived on the North Saskatchewan River in the 1780s, the Shoshoni had already retreated south, but they were still a favourite enemy of the Blackfoot tribes. Fur trade journals make several references to their battles. For example, at Manchester House in

1788 it was noted that the Peigans had arrived to trade and that "a number of them has been at war with and have killed 13 Snake Indians and are all going to war again this summer."

The Kootenay Indians dwelt on the west side of the Rocky Mountains, but at least one band, the Tuna'xe, lived in Alberta. They had come through the Crowsnest Pass and hunted along the foothills and out onto the plains. As one anthropologist noted:

> In winter they journeyed eastward well into the eastern foothills of south-western Alberta to hunt bison. Mostly, they seemed to have ranged between Crowsnest Lake and Waterton Lakes, but a number of their campsites extended east to the junction of the Oldman and Bow Rivers.
>
> This, and other hunts, were carried out on foot, supplemented with snowshoes during most of the winter season. At times they penetrated for some distance into the grasslands to pursue fleeing herds, to raid the Shoshoni Indians, or to visit friendly tribes, such as the Cree . . . the Blackfoot were not resident in the foothills at this time.

There is some question as to why they moved back across the mountains. Kootenay traditions tell about an early smallpox epidemic which virtually exterminated the band, while an elderly Blackfoot had a different story. "The Blackfeet hit the Kootenays," he said, "and drove them over the mountains. There were so many of them that they kept on retreating." In 1847, missionary Robert Rundle was told a similar story, that a major battle had started south of the Highwood River and the Kootenays "were chased about 40 or 50 miles to the south of this. The Peagans had guns but the Kootanies, &c. only 2 guns."

Whatever the cause, the Kootenays gave up their prairie life although in the generations that followed, they came out to the plains once or twice a year to hunt buffalo.

Information about the Crow Indians in southern Alberta is sketchy. One Indian commented "that the Crow Indians occupied the area south of the Bow River with other southern Indians and the Blackfoot were north of the Bow." They were said to have been driven out at the same time as the Shoshonis and Kootenays. However, they continued to make war against the Blackfoot and even after the Indians settled on their reserves in the 1880s, raids were taking place between the Blackfoot and the Crows, who by this time lived in south-eastern Montana.

With all three tribes, there is an unanswered question. Had they occupied southern Alberta for generations, only to be pushed out by the migrating Blackfoot in the 1700s? Or had the Blackfoot originally possessed those lands and been temporarily driven out because of some disaster, such as disease, starvation, or defeat in battle? Neither the Shoshoni, Kootenay nor Crow have any strong traditions about living in southern Alberta, so their period of residence in the area may have been of relatively short duration.

A Kootenay Indian visiting Fort Macleod was sketched in 1875 by a Mounted Policeman.

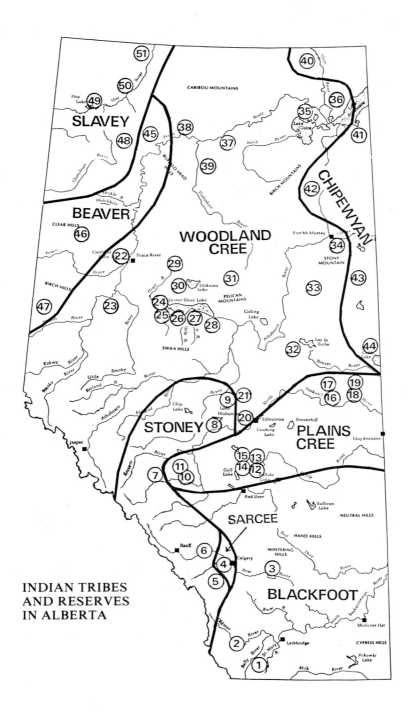

INDIAN TRIBES
AND RESERVES
IN ALBERTA

KEY TO RESERVES

Blackfoot
1. Blood
2. Peigan
3. Blackfoot

Sarcee
4. Sarcee

Stoney
5. Eden Valley
6. Stoney
7. Bighorn
8. Paul
9. Alexis

Plains Cree
10. Sunchild
11. O'Chiese*
12. Montana
13. Samson
14. Ermineskin
15. Louis Bull
16. Saddle Lake
17. Goodfish Lake
18. Frog Lake
19. Kehiwin

Woodland Cree
20. Enoch
21. Alexander
22. Duncan
23. Sturgeon Lake
24. Grouard
25. Sucker Creek
26. Driftpile

27. Swan River
28. Sawridge
29. Lubicon Lake
30. Whitefish Lake
31. Wabasca
32. Beaver Lake
33. Heart Lake
34. McMurray
35. Cree
36. Cree
37. Little Red River
38. Tallcree
39. Tallcree

Chipewyan
40. Fitz/Smith
41. Chipewyan
42. Fort McKay
43. Janvier
44. Cold Lake

Beaver
45. Boyer River
46. Clear Hills
47. Horse Hills

Slavey
48. Upper Hay River
49. Upper Hay River
50. Upper Hay River
51. Upper Hay River

* Although originally Ojibwa, this reserve is now equally divided between Cree and Ojibwa.

Sources Cited

Direct quotations used in this book can be found below. They are listed in the following sequence: page number, beginning words, and source. Full names of some authors and titles of books appear in the Further Reading List.

Blackfoot Nation: p.8, "very interesting people . . ." "Governor George Simpson's Journal, 1841," entry for March 24, 1841. Hudson's Bay Co. Archives; p.8, "very positive . . ." E. F. Wilson, "Report on the Blackfoot Tribes," *Third Report of the Committee, British Association for the Advancement of Science,* London, 1887, 12; p.9, "The War Chief. . ." Richard Glover, ed., *David Thompson's Narrative 1784-1812.* Toronto: The Champlain Society, 1962, 242; p.9, "our enemies . . ." Glover, 1962, 241-42; p.13, "The fiery water . . ." Morris, 1880, 248. **Blackfoot Tribe:** p.15, "If the Police . . ." Morris, 1880, 272; p.16, "alarmed them considerably . . ." Dempsey, 1972, 106; p. 16, "wheat was the only . . ." Annual Report, Department of Indian Affairs (hereafter DIA), 1884, 87; p.16, "From the beginning . . ." Dempsey, 1972, 191; p.19, "the Blackfoot has either . . ." *Calgary Herald,* Dec. 9, 1958. **Blood Tribe:** p.21, "Three years ago . . ." Morris, 1880, 273; p.21, "right to pursue . . ." Morris, 1880, 369; p. 23, "the Bloods think . . ." Annual Report, North-West Mounted Police, 1889, 42; p.24, "Give us ammunition . . ." Dempsey, 1980, 152; p.26, "This you can buy . . ." Dempsey, 1980, 216; p.26, "were opposed . . ." Hugh A. Dempsey, "Story of the Blood Reserve," *Alberta Historical Review,* 14:3 (November 1953) 35; p.26, "fraud, bribery and intimidation . . ." R. N. Wilson, *Our Betrayed Wards.* Ottawa: privately printed, 1921, 5. **Peigan Indians:** p.28, "about 200 lodges . . ." James Doty, "A Visit to the Blackfoot Camps," *Alberta Historical Review,* 14:3 (Summer 1966) 21; p.28, "on the Old Man's River . . ." Morris, 1880, 370; p.29, "cross ploughing . . ." Annual Report, DIA, 1880, 85; p.30, "These Indians are . . ." Annual Report, DIA, 1881, 117; p. 30, "no grain will mature . . ." Annual Report, DIA, 1894, 85; p.30, "Climatic conditions . . ." Annual Report, DIA, 1898, 160; p.32, "The water came over . . ." *Macleod Gazette,* Feb. 15, 1895; p.32, "I saw them pour . . ." *ibid.;* p.32, "I saw white men . . ." *ibid.;* p.32, "I have seen houses . . ." *ibid.;* p. 32, "If the old Peigan chiefs . . ." *ibid.;* p.32, "Little interest . . ." Annual Report, DIA, 1896, 194; p.33, "we looked down . . ." Walter McClintock, *The Old North Trail.* London: Macmillan and Co., 1910, 377; p.33, "the picturesque Indian camp . . ." *ibid.;* p.34, "It is obvious . . ." Maurice McDougall in *Pe-kun-nee,* Souvenir Program, Brocket, Alberta, 1975, 2.

Sarcee Indians: p.37, "These people have . . ." Elliott Coues, *New Light on the Early History of the Greater Northwest.* New York: Francis P. Harper, 1897, 737; p. 37, "on the south side . . ." Annual Report, DIA, 1881, p.xxv; p.38, "They said they were starving . . ." Letter, Indian Agent N. T. Macleod to Commissioner, Dec. 1, 1880 (copy in author's possession); p.38, "It took some days . . ." *Scarlet and Gold,* Fifth Annual, 1924, n.p.; p.39, "Their dislike . . ." Annual report of Indian Agent N. T. Macleod, Dec. 31, 1881 (copy in author's possession); p.39, "to have and to hold . . ." *Indian Treaties and Surrenders from 1680 to 1890.* Ottawa: King's Printer, 1905, vol.2, 138; p.39, "When work was begun . . ." Annual Report, DIA, 1884, 88; p.39, "there are some twelve . . ." *ibid.;* p.40, "To understand the difficulties . . ." Annual Report, DIA, 1895, 78; p.41, "We won't sell . . ." *Calgary Herald,* Feb. 4, 1913; p.41, "tuberculosis and trachoma . . . Memorandum, G. H. Gooderham to the author, 1962, Calgary Indian Mission Papers, M1356, f.6, Glenbow Archives; p.41, "All the children . . ." "Copy of Dr. Corbett's Report on the Sarcee School," Calgary Indian Mission Papers, M1356/f.6, Glenbow Archives. **Stoney Indians:** p.42, "that extensive track . . ." Glyndwr Williams, ed., *Andrew Graham's Observations on Hudson's Bay 1767-91.* London: Hudson's Bay Record Society, 1969, 193-94; p.42, "They are generally . . ." Coues, 1897, 516-17; p.42, "although the most arrant . . ." *ibid.;* p.43, "never frequent the plains . . ." Coues, 1897, 523; p.45, "We have been watching . . ." Morris, 1880, 266; p.46, "the Government considered . . ." Letter, M. Begg to Commissioner, May 19, 1886, RG-10, file 12349, Public Archives of Canada; p. 46, "the Stoney Indians are . . ." *Macleod Gazette,* Oct. 11, 1895. **Plains Cree:** p.50, "It was built . . ." Albert Tate, "A Winter Buffalo Hunt," *Alberta Historical Review,* 6:4 (Autumn 1958) 25; p.50, "While hunting . . ." Edwin Thompson Denig, *Five Indian Tribes of the Upper Missouri.* Norman: University of Oklahoma Press, 1961, 131; p.52, "in order to search . . ." Williams, 1969, 191; p.52, "Their unconquerable attachment . . ." Edward Umfreville, *The Present State of Hudson's Bay.* Toronto: Ryerson Press, 1954, 94; p.53, "Our country is getting ruined . . ." Morris, 1880, 171. **Woodland Cree:** p.57, "Either to avoid . . ." Williams, 1969, 191; p.58, "The nation is very numerous . . ." Williams, 1969, 193; p.58, "but also feared . . ." David C. Mandelbaum, *The Plains Cree.* Regina: Canadian Plains Research Center, 1979, 8; p.59, "had driven away the natives . . ." Alexander Mackenzie, *Voyages from Montreal.* Philadelphia: John Morgan, 1802, 139; p.59, "Their cloathing is made . . ." Robert Hood, "Some Account of the Cree and Other Indians, 1819," *Alberta Historical Review,* 15:1 (Winter 1967) 6; p.60, "Of all the nations . . ." Mackenzie, 1802, xc; p.61,

"They are so addicted . . ." Williams, 1969, 152; p.63, "Do you not allow . . ." Charles Mair, *Through the Mackenzie Basin.* Toronto: William Briggs, 1908, 60; p.63, "The Indians had no grain . . ." Annual Report, DIA, 1881, 84; p.63, "Their farming . . ." Annual Report, DIA, 1890, 52.
Chipewyan Indians: p.64, "pleased at having Goods . . ." W. Kaye Lamb, ed., *The Journals and Letters of Sir Alexander Mackenzie.* London: Cambridge University Press, 1970, 435; p.64, "sober, timorous and vagrant . . ." Mackenzie, 1802, cxiv; p.65, "The shrieks . . ." Williams, 1969, 198-99; p.66, "Thus arrayed . . ." Mackenzie, 1802, cxv; p.67, "Some ten or twelve . . ." William F. Butler, *The Wild North Land.* Toronto: Macmillan Co., 1910, 130; p.67, "drink no spiritous liquors . . ." Williams, 1969, 194; p.67, "As the people . . ." Mackenzie, 1802, cviii; p.67, "They are as much . . ." Hood, 1967, 16; p.67, "All the Indians . . ." *Treaty No. 8, Made June 21, 1899, and Adhesions, Reports, Etc.* Ottawa: Queen's Printer, 1957, 6; p.68, "The Chief . . ." *Treaty No. 8,* 1957, 3; p.68, "We proceeded . . ." Annual Report, DIA, 1908, 188; p.68, "They reported . . ." Annual Report, DIA, 1908, 71. **Beaver Indians:** p.71, "dwellers among beavers . . ." Frederick W. Hodge, *Handbook of American Indians North of Mexico.* Washington: Government Printing Service, 1907, II:822; p.71, "river of beavers . . ." *ibid.;* p.71, "When the country . . ." Mackenzie, 1802, 116; p.72, "differ very much . . ." Mackenzie, 1802, 142; p.72, "remained in the woods . . ." Pliny Earle Goddard, "The Beaver Indians," *Anthropological Papers of the American Museum of Natural History,* vol. x, pt.iv, 1916, 289; p.72, "No men in this land . . ." Butler, 1910, 175; p.73, "a peaceable . . ." Daniel Williams Harmon, *Sixteen Years in the Indian Country.* Toronto: Macmillan Co., 1957, 123; p.73, "are more vicious . . ." Mackenzie, 1802, 141; p.73, "They all rushed . . ." Goddard, 1916, 288; p.73, "their religion . . ." Mackenzie, 1802, 141; p.74, "the great part . . ." Harmon, 1957, 123; p.74, "On the morning . . ." Butler, 1910, 175-76; p.75, "The Indians . . ." *Treaty No. 8,* 1957, 6; p.76, "temperate and fairly moral . . ." Annual Report, DIA, 1913, 192; p.76, "they do not progress . . ." *ibid.* **Slavey Indians:** p.78, "Their summer dress . . ." L. R. Masson, *Les Bourgeois de la Compagnie du Nord-Ouest.* Quebec: A. Cote & Co., 1890, II:92; p.78, "The tender sex . . ." *ibid.;* p.79, "They live in lodges . . ." Masson, 1890, II:91; p.80, "There are many natives . . ." Williams, 1969, 200-01; p.81, "The Indians on the north . . ." Annual Report, DIA, 1902, 178; p.24, "At that place . . ." C. B. Osgoode, "The Ethnography of the Great Bear Lake Indians," *Annual Report for 1931, National Museum of Canada, Bulletin No. 70.* Ottawa: King's Printer, 1932, 31; p.82, "Round his own district . . ." *Edmonton Journal,* Oct. 9, 1929; p.82, "Their dispositions . . ." Masson, 1890, 1:89.

Ojibwa Indians: p.83, "These Indians . . ." Johnson, 1967, 6n; p.83, "The Bungee Indians traded . . ." Johnson, 1967, 114; p.83, "some few of . . ." *ibid.;* p.84, "Several of the . . ." Robert T. Rundle, *The Rundle Journals, 1840-1848.* Calgary: Historical Society of Alberta, 1977, 50; p.85, "They say . . ." Letter, S. B. Lucas to Indian Commissioner, Feb. 24, 1885. RG-10, vol. 3707, file 19,240, PAC; p.85, "as then those . . ." Letter, John A. Macdonald to Indian Commissioner, March 11, 1885. RG-10, vol. 3707, file 19,240, PAC; p.85, "Forty lodges . . ." *Calgary Tribune,* Sept. 23, 1887; p.85, "In this district . . ." *Edmonton Bulletin,* Nov. 11, 1901; p.86 "very old . . ." *ibid.;* p.87, "All our lives . . ." *The Mountaineer,* Rocky Mountain House, July 16, 1959. **Iroquois Indians:** p.88, "Nepissings, the Algonquins . . ." Glover, 1962, 156; p.88, "now spread themselves . . ." *ibid.;* p.88, "to complete . . ." Alice M. Johnson, *Saskatchewan Journals and Correspondence.* London: Hudson's Bay Record Society, 1967, xcii; p.88, "For several years . . ." Harmon, 1957, 193; p.90, "they bought a . . ." C. L. Johnstone, *Winter and Summer Excursions in Canada.* London: Digby, Long & Co., 1894, 107-08; p.90, "I passed fifteen . . ." *idem,* 109-10; p.91, "The crops . . ." Annual Report, DIA, 1884, 146; p.91, "These men are not . . ." Victoria Callihoo, "The Iroquois in Alberta," *Alberta Historical Review,* 7:2 (Spring 1959) 17-18; p.91, "Thirteen families . . ." James Gibbons, "Iroquois in the North West Territories," *Annual Archaeological Report 1903.* Toronto: King's Printer, 1904, 126. **Gros Ventre Indians:** p.92, "three or four . . ." Johnson, 1967, 311; p.92, "and that they will . . ." *idem,* 321. **Shoshoni, Kootenay and Crow Indians:** p.94, "The Blackfeet . . ." Interview with Jim White Bull, Blood Indian, by the author, July 22, 1954; p.94, "the battles . . ." Glover, 1962, 49; p.94, "The opposing forces . . ." John C. Ewers, "A Blood Indian's Conception of Tribal Life in Dog Days," *The Blue Jay,* 17:1 (March 1960) 47; p.95, "a number of them . . ." Manchester House Journals, entry for March 25, 1788. A/11/117, Hudson's Bay Co. Archives; p.95, "In winter . . ." Claude E. Schaeffer, "Plains Kutenai: An Ethnological Evaluation," *Alberta History,* 30:4 (Autumn 1982) 5; p.95, "The Blackfeet . . ." Interview with Jim White Bull, *op. cit.;* p.95, "were chased . . ." Rundle, 1977, 264; p.95, "that the Crow . . ." Interview with Bobtail Chief, Blood Indian, by the author, Summer 1952.

Photographs: All photographs are from the Glenbow Archives, except for the following: National Archives, Washington, D.C., 10; National Museum of Canada, Ottawa, 17; Public Archives of Canada, Ottawa, 20, 27 (top) 90; Pollard Collection, Provincial Archives of Alberta, Edmonton, 36; Royal Ontario Museum, Toronto, 43; and Walters Art Gallery, Baltimore, 88.

FURTHER READING

Besides the books quoted in this volume, there are other works which deal with Alberta tribes. Below are listed some of the most useful ones.

Barbeau, Marius, *Indian Days on the Western Prairies*. Ottawa: National Museum of Canada, Bulletin No. 163, 1960.

Dempsey, Hugh A., *Crowfoot, Chief of the Blackfeet*. Norman: University of Oklahoma Press, 1972.

Dempsey, Hugh A., *Red Crow, Warrior Chief*. Saskatoon: Western Producer Prairie Books, 1980.

Ewers, John C. *The Horse in Blackfoot Indian Culture*. Washington: Smithsonian Institution, 1955.

Ewers, John C., *The Blackfeet, Raiders on the Northwestern Plains*. Norman: University of Oklahoma Press, 1958.

Getty, Ian A. L., and Donald B. Smith, eds., *One Century Later; Western Canadian Reserve Indians Since Treaty 7*. Vancouver: UBC Press, 1978.

Grinnell, George Bird, *Blackfoot Lodge Tales*. Lincoln: University of Nebraska Press, 1962.

Jenness, Diamond, *Indians of Canada*. Ottawa: National Museum of Canada, Bulletin 65, 1969.

Mandelbaum, David G., *The Plains Cree*. Regina: Canadian Plains Research Centre, 1979.

Morris, Alexander, *The Treaties of Canada, with the Indians of Manitoba and the North-West Territories*. Toronto: Willing and Williamson, 1880.

Mountain Horse, Mike, *My People the Bloods*. Calgary: Glenbow Museum, 1979.

Price, Richard, ed., *The Spirit of the Alberta Indian Treaties*. Montreal: Institute for Research on Public Policy, 1980.

Snow, Chief John, *These Mountains are our Sacred Places*. Toronto: Samuel Stevens, 1977.